Success in English Literature

WITHDRAWN

Steven Croft
Helen Cross

OXFORD
UNIVERSITY PRESS

OXFORD

UNIVERSITY PRESS

Great Clarendon Street, Oxford OX2 6DP

Oxford University Press is a department of the University of Oxford.
It furthers the University's objective of excellence in research, scholarship,
and education by publishing worldwide in

Oxford New York

Auckland Bangkok Buenos Aires Cape Town Chennai
Dar es Salaam Delhi Hong Kong Istanbul Karachi Kolkata
Kuala Lumpur Madrid Melbourne Mexico City Mumbai Nairobi
São Paulo Shanghai Taipei Tokyo Toronto

Oxford is a registered trade mark of Oxford University Press
in the UK and in certain other countries

A CIP catalogue record for this book is available from the British Library

ISBN 0 19 831480 9

10 9 8 7 6 5 4 3 2

Designed by Mike Brain Graphic Design Limited, Oxford

Typeset by AFS Image Setters Ltd, Glasgow

Printed in Great Britain by Alden Press Ltd, Oxford

Orders and enquiries to Customer Services:
Tel: 01536 741068   Fax: 01536 454519

Contents

Acknowledgements

The authors and publisher are grateful for permission to reprint the following copyright material:

Chinua Achebe: extract from *Things Fall Apart* (Heinemann, 1962), reprinted by permission of Reed Educational & Professional Publishing.

John Agard: 'Listen Mr Oxford Don' from *Mangoes and Bullets: Selected and New Poems 1972-84*, (Pluto Press, 1985), reprinted by permission of the present publisher, Serpent's Tail Ltd.

Moniza Alvi: 'Hindi Urdu Bol Chaal' from *A Bowl of Warm Air* (OUP, 1996)

Kingsley Amis: extract from *Lucky Jim* (Victor Gollancz), reprinted by permission of The Orion Publishing Group Ltd.

W. H. Auden: 'Twelve Songs IX' from *The Collected Poems of W. H. Auden* (Faber & Faber), reprinted by permission of the publisher.

Valerie Bloom: 'Language Barrier' from *Touch mi, Tell mi* (Bogle L' Ouverture Press, 1983), reprinted by permission of the author.

Elizabeth Bowen: extract from 'The Little Girl's Room' from *The Collected Stories of Elizabeth Bowen*, copyright © 1980 Curtis Brown Ltd, Literary Executors of the Estate of Elizabeth Bowen, reprinted by permission of Curtis Brown Ltd, London.

Bill Bryson: extract from *Notes From a Small Island* (Black Swan, 1996), reprinted by permission of Transworld Publishers.

Wendy Cope: 'Making Cocoa for Kingsley Amis', 'Reading Scheme', 'A Nursery Rhyme (as it might have been written by William Wordsworth)' and 'A Nursery Rhyme (as it might have been written by T. S. Eliot)', all from *Making Cocoa for Kingsley Amis* (Faber & Faber, 1986), reprinted by permission of the publisher.

Jenny Diski: extract from *Skating to Antarctica* (Granta, 1997), reprinted by permission of the publisher.

Keith Douglas: 'Vergissmeinicht' from *The Collected Poems of Keith Douglas* (Faber & Faber) reprinted by permission of the publisher.

Carol Ann Duffy: 'We Remember Your Childhood Well' from *The Other Country* (Anvil Press Poetry, 1990, 1998), reprinted by permission of the publisher.

Brian Friel: extract from *Translations* (Faber & Faber, 1981), reprinted by permission of the publisher.

John Galsworthy: Extracts from *Strife* (Duckworth, 1980)

Tony Harrison: 'A Cold Coming' from *The Gaze of the Gorgon* (Bloodaxe Books, 1992)

Seamus Heaney: 'Mid-Term Break' from *Death of a Naturalist* (Faber & Faber), reprinted by permission of the publisher.

Ted Hughes: 'Thrushes' from *Lupercal* (Faber & Faber), reprinted by permission of the publisher.

Evan Jones: 'The Song of the Banana Man' and 'The Lament of the Banana Man' from *Penguin Book of Caribbean Verse*

Philip Larkin: 'Love Songs in Age' from *The Whitsun Weddings* (Faber & Faber, 1964); 'The Explosion' from *High Windows* (Faber & Faber, 1974), both reprinted by permission of the publisher.

D. H. Lawrence: extract from *Sons and Lovers* (Penguin Books); extracts from *The Rainbow* (Penguin Books); both reprinted by permission of Laurence Pollinger Ltd and the Estate of Frieda Lawrence Ravagli.

Peter Mathiessen: extract from *The Snow Leopard* (Chatto & Windus, 1979), reprinted by permission of The Random House Group Ltd.

Edna St Vincent Millay: 'Time Does Not Bring Relief' from *Collected Poems* (HarperCollins, 1917, 1945), copyright © Edna St Vincent Millay 1917, 1945, reprinted by permission of Elizabeth Barnett, Literary Executor.

Edwin Muir: 'The Horses' from *The Collected Poems of Edwin Muir* (Faber & Faber), reprinted by permission of the publisher.

George Orwell: extract from *Down and Out in Paris and London* (Secker & Warburg, 1933), copyright © George Orwell 1933, reprinted by permission of A. M. Heath on behalf of Bill Hamilton as the Literary Executor of the Estate of the Late Sonia Brownell Orwell.

John Pilger: 'The Miners' from *Distant Voices* (Vintage, 1992), reprinted by permission of David Higham Associates Ltd.

Karl Shapiro: 'Auto Wreck' from *Collected Poems 1940–1978*

Theatre Workshop: extract from *Oh What a Lovely War*, revised and restored to the original version by Joan Littlewood (Methuen, 1965), copyright © Joan Littlewood Productions 1965, reprinted by permission of the publisher.

Ngugi wa Thiong'o: Extract from *Decolonising the Mind: The Politics of Language in African Literature* (James Currey, 1981)

Dylan Thomas: 'And Death Shall Have No Dominion' and 'Do Not Go Gentle Into That Good Night' from *The Collected Poems* (J. M. Dent), reprinted by permission of David Higham Associates Ltd.

Virginia Woolf: 'A Sketch of the Past' from *Moments of Being* edited by Schulkind (Hogarth Press, 1989), reprinted by permission of The Random House Group on behalf of the executors of the Virginia Woolf Estate.

We are also grateful to the following students for allowing us to use their responses as examples: Sandra Haigh, Emma Hallas, L. P. Jordison, Michael Lomas, Olwen Robson, David Simpson.

Although we have tried to trace and contact copyright holders before publication, in some cases this has not been possible. If contacted we will be pleased to rectify any errors or omissions at the earliest opportunity.

Introduction

This text has been specially written to support the AS and A2 specifications in English Literature. Although different Examination Boards have approached the common Assessment Objectives in different ways, some kind of 'unseen' work is required by all Boards. This book is designed to help you prepare for that kind of task, whatever specific form it may take. It also provides many opportunities for you to develop general literary awareness and to practise the skills of close reading.

Close reading

Close reading is the art of paying attention to details of language and structure in order to come to the best possible understanding of texts and of how writers create meaning. When you are asked to analyse texts or extracts you are meeting for the first time, whether or not this is in an examination, the more you have developed the habit and skills of close reading, the more you will be able to discover for yourself about the text.

There are some methods and some ways of planning your approach which can help you feel more confident about the close reading of unprepared texts.

First, it is important not to be daunted by poems or prose extracts you are given to analyse. There will be good reasons why a particular piece has been chosen, and with close reading you will be able to discover them.

It is helpful to have a strategy which will allow you to examine any text in detail. Below is a checklist of the things you need to consider as you read it. As this list suggests, it is a good idea to begin with an overview or general point, such as the theme of the text, and go on to look at the details. A written response, such as a 'critical appreciation' of a poem, can be structured in this way too.

- **Subject or theme** What is the text about? This may seem too obvious, but it is a good broad starting point. What other information do you have, for example the writer's name or a date?
- **Speaker and/or situation** Whose 'voice' do you hear in the text? Is it written in the third person or the first person? If it is first-person writing, is the voice that of the author, or is the writer taking on a role? In poems, in particular, writers can sometimes adopt not only the voices of characters, but the 'voice' of an object (for example a mountain or the wind), an animal, or even a god. Decide to whom the text is addressed, and the situation in which it is set.
- **Form** What is the overall structure of the piece? For example, is it in a

recognizable poetic form? Are there any obvious ways in which it could be divided into sections, either by its layout, its meaning, or by changes in the way language is presented at different points?

- **Ideas and messages** Look for ideas that are embedded 'below the surface' of the text. Think about the author's aims and purposes. Are there any signs of irony or satire? (See Unit 2 for examples.)
- **Tone and atmosphere** How would you describe the writer's 'tone of voice'? Is there an atmosphere or feeling pervading the text, such as sadness, anger, or joy? If so, what is it about the writing that creates this effect? (For example, long sentences, with soft consonant sounds and repeated use of 'oo' and 'o' vowels, tend to create a sombre effect.)
- **Imagery** What kinds of visual images or 'word-pictures' does the text present? How does the writer use simile or metaphor? Comment on both individual examples and on patterns of images which you notice. Be careful to explain and analyse these examples in terms of their contribution to the overall meaning of the text.
- **Vocabulary** What do you notice about the individual words and phrases the writer has chosen? Do certain types of words recur? For example, there may be clusters of words relating to themes such as death, or fire, or childhood. Are there words that seem unexpected or out of place? What effect do they create?
- **Rhyme, rhythm, and sound effects** With a poem, examine the rhyme-scheme, if any, and its effect. Beware of simply describing a rhyme-scheme without going on to say why you think the poet has chosen it and how far this aim is achieved. Rhythm can be important in prose as well as in poetry. Are the sentences flowing or short and jerky? Does the rhythm change at key points in the text? Other sound effects or aural images are created through the use of devices like alliteration. Remember to comment on the *effect* of these. If you cannot see any particular effect, it is better not to mention these features at all.
- **Conclusion** Finally, return to an overview of the text. Sum up how the effects and details of style you have analysed come together to create a 'whole' piece of writing. How has your reading of it contributed to your understanding of the subject that it deals with? Does the text offer a way of looking at things that you had not considered before? If the question invites you to give a personal response to the text, this is the place to do it.

This list is *not* intended as a formula to be applied rigidly in every situation. Not every unseen text requires detailed analysis of every one of these points. However, this checklist can act as a starting point from which to organize your thoughts.

As well as analysing individual unseen texts in detail, you are very likely to be asked to work with two or more texts, making comparisons and connections. You may also be required to show that you have developed an awareness of the different contexts in which literature is written, such as different historical periods or literary traditions, and the ways in which these might affect a writer's work.

How to use this book

The various texts selected here have been grouped under general thematic headings, which is an approach taken by some Examination Boards. You will find much valuable practice here – each Unit contains a range of texts from a variety of periods and genres, accompanied by structured activities. Early on in many Units you will find some general feedback on the tasks, but this has been deliberately omitted from later activities so as not to influence your responses unduly. In each Unit you will also find a student response to one or more of the activities, and this is accompanied by some comments indicating the qualities of each answer from an examiner's point of view.

The activities have been designed to develop and test your ability to:
* Communicate clearly
* Respond with knowledge and understanding to literary texts of different types and periods
* Explore and comment on the relationships and comparisons between texts
* Show detailed understanding of the ways in which the writers' choices of form, structure and language shape meanings
* Articulate independent judgements informed by different interpretations of literary texts by other readers
* Evaluate the significance of cultural, historical and other contextual influences upon literary texts.

Of course, not all the activities can test all these objectives at the same time, but working on a selection of them will help to prepare you for whatever unseen passages, poems or other extracts you may have to face in the exam. We hope you will enjoy using this book, and that it will contribute to your *success*.

1

'Nature, Red in Tooth and Claw'?

Writers and thinkers have always been intrigued by 'nature' and have wondered about just where the human race fits in with it. Our human consciousness and self-awareness appear to separate us from the natural world. To what extent are we outsiders, observers looking in, and to what extent are we part of the whole picture? Is nature benign, and does it constitute our true home, or is it something wild and hostile, which has to be 'tamed'?

Thinking about what 'nature' is, or what is 'natural', in itself raises questions, as in order to define 'nature' we need something outside it or separate from it, something 'unnatural' or 'artificial', perhaps, with which it can be contrasted. Commonly, things that are created or tampered with by human beings are seen as unnatural – but if humans are themselves part of the natural order, is this necessarily so? For example, what is the difference between a wasps' nest, which is considered 'natural', and a town, which is not? In particular, what is the relationship between art, including literature, and nature?

Over time, and in different contexts, writers' responses to questions about nature and art have varied widely. Following is a sample of some of the viewpoints to look out for when you read texts focusing on these themes.

- In medieval literature, Nature is often personified as a goddess, either the Universal Mother of all creation in her own right, or one who carries out the work of creation on God's behalf. Here, for example, is a speech from Chaucer's *Physician's Tale*, in which he imagines Nature boasting of the power that has enabled her to create a noble virgin:

  > Lo! I, Nature,
  > Thus kan I forme and peynte a creature,
  > Whan that me list; who kan me countrefete?
  > Pigmalion noght, though he ay forge and bete,
  > Or grave, or peynte, for I dar wel seyn,
  > Apelles, Zanzis, sholde werche in veyn
  > Outher to grave, or peynte, or forge, or bete,
  > If they presumed me to countrefete.
  > For He that is the formere principal

Hath maked me his vicaire general,
To forme and peynten erthely creaturis
Right as me list, and ech thyng in my cure is
Under the moone, that may wane and waxe;
And for my werk right no thyng wol I axe;
My lord and I been ful of oon accord.
I made hire to the worship of my lord;
So do I alle myne othere creatures,
What colour that they han, or what figures.

Geoffrey Chaucer

- Some Augustan writers suggest that true art is not separate from nature. Where humans create things sensitively and in good taste, they are in harmony with nature.
- For Wordsworth, nature was something spiritual; it nurtures body, spirit and imagination, and is the inspiration for his art. This is considered to be the 'Romantic' view of nature, although other poets of the Romantic era did not entirely share his point of view.
- Some mainstream Victorian writers tend to see nature as blind or mechanistic and indifferent to human life, hence Tennyson's phrase, 'Nature, Red in tooth and claw'. For Emily Brontë, on the other hand, nature is the source of life and her spiritual home.
- Thomas Hardy celebrates the sacred beauty of nature, but from the pessimistic viewpoint that it is inaccessible and cannot be shared by human beings.
- Twentieth-century writers, such as D. H. Lawrence and Ted Hughes, explore what they see as the increasing alienation of western culture from the natural world. Others explore the damaging impact on nature of human 'progress'.

ACTIVITY   Before you read the texts in this unit, discuss some of these questions and ideas and compare your own beliefs and assumptions about 'nature'.

It is also important to think about the ways in which writers may use language to convey their ideas about nature. For example:

- **Imagery** is often very significant. Writers often use simile and metaphor when they attempt to portray or 'capture' an aspect of nature in writing. Metaphors from the natural world are regularly used to explore aspects of human life and experience.
- Writers often draw **parallels** or **contrasts** between human life and nature.
- Look out for **anthropomorphism**, where writers attribute human characteristics to things that are not human, e.g. landscapes, trees, animals or the Earth itself. Where animals are assumed to share human thoughts or emotions, this is sometimes also referred to as the **'pathetic fallacy'**. This term was coined by John Ruskin in 1856, and relates to the Greek word *pathos* meaning 'feeling' or 'suffering'.

• Writers' views on what is 'natural' may be reflected in their **style**. They may, for example, choose simple vocabulary and free-flowing sentence structures or poetic forms – rather than complex words and images, tightly constructed sentences or elaborate verse forms.

Our first two texts are by poets for whom nature is essentially benign and the spiritual source of their inspiration.

The Prelude

In his long poem *The Prelude*, William Wordsworth – who is regarded as the quintessential Romantic poet of nature – tells the story of his life, pausing, sometimes, to reflect on significant moments. In addition to believing that the natural world should be the most important source of inspiration for poetry, Wordsworth felt that there can be certain moments in our lives in which we go beyond, or transcend, everyday 'reality' and experience ourselves and the world around us more vividly or in a different way. These 'spots of time', as he calls them, stand out in our memories and have the power to strengthen us in difficult times. For him, his childhood in the English Lake District was particularly rich in these moments, many of which are recorded in the first books of *The Prelude*. Here he describes the experience of skating on a frozen lake at nightfall.

ACTIVITY Read the following extract carefully, alone or with a partner. Discuss and make notes about these questions:
1 How does Wordsworth use language and imagery to convey a) the landscape and weather; b) movement and sound; c) his own feelings?
2 In what ways does the second section contrast with the first?
3 In the third section, what is Wordsworth saying about Nature and its effect on his own life?

And in the frosty season, when the sun
Was set, and visible for many a mile
The cottage windows through the twilight blazed,
I heeded not the summons; happy time
It was indeed for all of us, to me
It was a time of rapture. Clear and loud
The village clock tolled six; I wheeled about
Proud and exulting, like an untired horse
That cares not for its home. All shod with steel
We hissed along the polished ice in games
Confederate, imitative of the chace
And woodland pleasures, the resounding horn,
The pack loud bellowing, and the hunted hare.

So through the darkness and the cold we flew,
And not a voice was idle. With the din,
Meanwhile, the precipices rang aloud;
The leafless trees and every icy crag
Tinkled like iron, while the distant hills
Into the tumult sent an alien sound
Of melancholy, not unnoticed, while the stars,
Eastward, were sparkling clear, and in the west
The orange sky of evening died away.

    Not seldom from the uproar I retired
Into a silent bay, or sportively
Glanced sideways, leaving the tumultuous throng,
To cut across the image of a star
That gleamed upon the ice. And oftentimes
When we had given our bodies to the wind,
And all the shadowy banks on either side
Came sweeping through the darkness, spinning still
The rapid line of motion, then at once
Have I, reclining back upon my heels,
Stopped short – yet still the solitary cliffs
Wheeled by me, even as if the earth had rolled
With visible motion her diurnal round.
Behind me did they stretch in solemn train,
Feebler and feebler, and I stood and watched
Till all was tranquil as a dreamless sleep.

    Ye presences of Nature, in the sky
Or on the earth, ye visions of the hills
And souls of lonely places, can I think
A vulgar hope was yours when ye employed
Such ministry – when ye through many a year
Haunting me thus among my boyish sports,
On caves and trees, upon the woods and hills,
Impressed upon all forms the characters
Of danger or desire, and thus did make
The surface of the universal earth
With triumph, and delight, and hope, and fear,
Work like a sea?

William Wordsworth

Here are some of the points you may have noticed:

- Wordsworth's vocabulary and imagery is vivid and powerful. The sky is 'orange' and 'the twilight blazed'; the sounds are 'clear and loud', with the skaters 'hissing' on the ice and 'bellowing' like a pack of hounds. He feels not just happiness, but 'rapture' and he conveys his childhood sensation of excitement and boundless energy by comparing himself to 'an untired horse' which 'wheeled about/Proud and exulting'.

- In the second section, he leaves the 'pack' and is alone with nature. Coming to a sudden halt after his energetic motion, he has the sense that it is now the landscape which is 'spinning' and 'wheeling' around him. He watches and waits as that feeling fades into stillness and tranquillity.

- In the third section, he personifies Nature as spirits or 'presences', to which he attributes a deliberate wish to 'haunt' him. The feelings, of 'triumph, and delight, and hope, and fear', which he experiences in 'spots of time' like this, are so powerful that he projects them onto the natural world: it is as if the landscape itself carries those feelings and he can never again see it without experiencing them afresh.

High Waving Heather

Emily Brontë is best known for her novel *Wuthering Heights*, but she also wrote many poems, often drawing inspiration from the wild landscape of the Yorkshire moors, where she lived all her short life. This one was written in December 1836.

High waving heather, 'neath stormy blasts bending,
  Midnight and moonlight and bright shining stars:
Darkness and glory rejoicingly blending,
Earth rising to heaven and heaven descending;
Man's spirit away from the drear dungeon sending, –
  Bursting the fetters and breaking the bars.

All down the mountain-sides wild forests lending
  One mighty voice to the life-giving wind;
Rivers their banks in the jubilee rending,
Fast through the valleys a reckless course wending,
  Leaving a desolate desert behind.

Shining and lowering and swelling and dying, –
  Changing for ever, from midnight to noon;
Roaring like thunder, like soft music sighing,
Shadows on shadows advancing and flying,
Lightning-bright flashes the deep gloom defying,
  Coming as swiftly and fading as soon.

Emily Brontë

ACTIVITY   1 Read the poem carefully and make notes on how Brontë uses language to describe the landscape and the weather.

2 What impression does she give of the natural world and of her own feelings and response to it?
3 What is her view of the relationship between nature and the human spirit?
4 Using your notes, write a short critical appreciation of the poem.
5 Write an essay in which you compare and contrast the ways in which Wordsworth and Brontë describe landscapes and weather, and explore how each is inspired by nature in texts A and B.

King Lear

In the tragedy *King Lear*, Shakespeare presents a less appealing view of the natural world. The elderly Lear has divided his kingdom between his two older daughters, Goneril and Regan. His third daughter, Cordelia, the most loyal of the three, was unwilling to *appear* dutiful enough to deserve her share, and has been disinherited. He soon discovers that he has made a terrible mistake. Neither of the older daughters will treat him with the respect and consideration he requires. Mad with grief and rage, he takes to the moors in a storm, accompanied by two faithful followers: the Duke of Kent, who has also met with Lear's disapproval and is in disguise as a servant, and Lear's Fool, or jester. On the heath, they encounter Edgar, son of the Duke of Gloucester, who is also in disguise in order to protect himself. Edgar is pretending to be the mad beggar, 'Poor Tom.'

Act III Scene 4

(*The heath. Before a hovel*
Enter **Lear**, **Kent**, *and* **Fool**)

Kent: Here is the place, my Lord; good my Lord, enter:
The tyranny of the open night's too rough
For nature to endure.   (*Storm still*)

Lear: Let me alone.

Kent: Good my Lord, enter here.

Lear: Wilt break my heart?

Kent: I had rather break mine own. Good my Lord, enter.

Lear: Thou think'st 'tis much that this contentious storm
Invades us to the skin: so 'tis to thee;
But where the greater malady is fixed,
The lesser is scarce felt. Thou'ldst shun a bear;
But if thy flight lay toward the roaring sea,
Thou'ldst meet the bear i'th'mouth. When the mind's free
The body's delicate; this tempest in my mind
Doth from my senses take all feeling else
Save what beats there – filial ingratitude!

Is it not as this mouth should tear this hand
For lifting food to't? But I will punish home:
No, I will weep no more. In such a night
To shut me out? Pour on; I will endure,
In such a night as this? O Regan, Goneril!
Your old kind father, whose frank heart gave all, –
O! that way madness lies; let me shun that;
No more of that.

Kent: Good my Lord, enter here.

Lear: Prithee, go in thyself; seek thine own ease:
This tempest will not give me leave to ponder
On things would hurt me more. But I'll go in.
(*To the* **Fool**) In, boy; go first. (*Kneeling*) You houseless poverty, –
Nay, get thee in. I'll pray, and then I'll sleep.

(**Fool** *goes in*)

Poor naked wretches, whereso'er you are,
That bide the pelting of this pitiless storm,
How shall your houseless heads and unfed sides,
Your looped and windowed raggedness, defend you
From seasons such as these? O! I have ta'en
Too little care of this. Take physic, Pomp;
Expose thyself to feel what wretches feel,
That thou mayst shake the superflux to them,
And show the Heavens more just.

Edgar: (*Within*) Fathom and half, fathom and half!
Poor Tom!   (*The* **Fool** *runs out from the hovel*)

Fool: Come not in here, Nuncle; here's a spirit.
Help me! help me!

Kent: Give me thy hand. Who's there?

Fool: A spirit, a spirit: he says his name's Poor Tom.

Kent: What art thou that dost grumble there i'th'straw?
Come forth.

(*Enter* **Edgar** *disguised as a madman*)

Edgar: Away! the foul fiend follows me! Through the
sharp hawthorn blow the cold winds. Humh! go to
thy bed and warm thee.

Lear: Didst thou give all to thy daughters?
And art come to this?

Edgar: Who gives any thing to poor Tom? whom the
foul fiend hath led through fire and through flame,
through ford and whirlpool, o'er bog and
quagmire; that hath laid knives under his pillow,
and halters in his pew; set ratsbane by his porridge;
made him proud of heart, to ride on a bay
trotting-horse over four-inched bridges, to course
his own shadow for a traitor. Bless thy five wits!
Tom's a-cold. O! do de, do de. Bless thee

	from whirlwinds, star-blasting, and taking! Do Poor
	Tom some charity, whom the foul fiend vexes.
	There could I have him now, and there, and there
	again, and there. *(Storm still)*
Lear:	What! has his daughters brought him to this pass?
	(To **Edgar***)* Couldst thou save nothing? Would'st thou give 'em all?
Fool:	Nay, he reserved a blanket, else we had all been shamed.
Lear:	Now all the plagues that in the pendulous air
	Hang fated o'er men's faults light on thy daughters!
Kent:	He hath no daughters, Sir.
Lear:	Death, traitor! nothing could have subdued nature
	To such a lowness but his unkind daughters.
	Is it the fashion that discarded fathers
	Should have thus little mercy on their flesh?
	Judicious punishment! 'twas this flesh begot
	Those pelican daughters.
Edgar:	Pillicock sat on Pillicock hill:
	Alow, alow, loo, loo!
Fool:	This cold night will turn us all to fools and madmen.
Edgar:	Take heed o'th'foul fiend. Obey thy parents; keep
	thy word justly; swear not; commit not with man's
	sworn spouse; set not thy sweet heart on proud
	array. Tom's a-cold.
Lear:	What hast thou been?
Edgar:	A servingman, proud in heart and mind; that curled
	my hair, wore gloves in my cap, served the lust of
	my mistress' heart, and did the act of darkness with
	her; swore as many oaths as I spake words,
	and broke them in the sweet face of Heaven; one
	that slept in the contriving of lust, and waked to do
	it. Wine loved I deeply, dice dearly, and in woman
	out-paramoured the Turk; false of heart, light of
	ear, bloody of hand; hog in sloth, fox in stealth,
	wolf in greediness, dog in madness, lion in prey.
	Let not the creaking of shoes nor the rustling of
	silks betray thy poor heart to woman: keep thy foot
	out of brothels, thy hand out of plackets, thy pen
	from lenders' books, and defy the foul fiend. Still
	through the hawthorn blows the cold wind;
	says suum, mun, hey no nonny. Dolphin my boy,
	boy; sessa! let him trot by. *(Storm still)*
Lear:	Thou wert better in a grave than to answer with
	thy uncovered body this extremity of the skies. Is
	man no more than this? Consider him well.
	Thou ow'st the worm no silk, the beast no hide,
	the sheep no wool, the cat no perfume. Ha! here's
	three on's are sophisticated; thou art the thing

itself; unaccommodated man is no more but such a
poor, bare, forked animal as thou art. Off, off,
you lendings! Come; unbutton here.   (*Tearing off his clothes*)

William Shakespeare

1 Shakespeare here contrasts human life in its 'natural', most basic state, with the 'civilized' life to which Lear has been hitherto accustomed. Make two lists of details from the text which illustrate the comparison. You will find some examples in Edgar's speeches as well as Lear's, even though Edgar is pretending to be mad and therefore deliberately talking 'nonsense'. There is more hidden sense in Lear's genuine 'madness', though.

2 What view of the 'natural world' do we gain here from references to the weather and to animals?

3 In what ways does Lear's last speech in the extract differ from his earlier ones? Why, do you think?

4 Although Lear is 'mad' at this point in the play, his words reveal that he learns something and is changed as a result of his exposure to the storm and his encounter with 'Poor Tom'. Discuss and make notes on how this is shown in his speeches in the extract. (If you are familiar with the play, relate your ideas to your understanding of the whole text.)

5 King Lear is a play about 'what it means to be human'. Write an assessment of the extract focusing on how this theme is presented here.

Next, three 'nature' poets of different eras respond to similar subject matter but reflect on it in different ways to create poems with a variety of messages about nature and human life.

The Thrush's Nest

John Clare (1793–1864) was a contemporary of the major Romantic poets and is usually regarded as a 'fringe' member of the group. Nature and the rural environment provide most of his material and he writes in a direct, unselfconscious manner.

Within a thick and spreading hawthorn bush
   That overhung a mole-hill large and round,
I heard from morn to morn a merry thrush
   Sing hymns to sunrise, while I drank the sound
With joy; and, often an intruding guest,
   I watched her secret toils from day to day –
How true she warped the moss to form a nest,
   And modelled it within with wood and clay;
And by and by, like heath-bells gilt with dew,

There lay her shining eggs, as bright as flowers,
Ink-spotted over shells of greeny blue;
   And there I witnessed, in the sunny hours,
A brood of nature's minstrels chirp and fly,
Glad as that sunshine and the laughing sky.

John Clare

A song thrush feeding young in the nest

The Darkling Thrush

31 December 1900

I leant upon a coppice gate
   When Frost was spectre-grey
And Winter's dregs made desolate
   The weakening eye of day.
The tangled bine-stems scored the sky
   Like strings of broken lyres,
And all mankind that haunted nigh
   Had sought their household fires.

The land's sharp features seemed to be
   The Century's corpse outleant,
His crypt the cloudy canopy,
   The wind his death-lament.
The ancient pulse of germ and birth
   Was shrunken hard and dry,
And every spirit upon earth
   Seemed fervourless as I.

At once a voice arose among
   The bleak twigs overhead

In a full-hearted evensong
   Of joy illimited;
An aged thrush, frail, gaunt, and small,
   In blast-beruffled plume,
Had chosen thus to fling his soul
   Upon the growing gloom.

So little cause for carolings
   Of such ecstatic sound
Was written on terrestrial things
   Afar or nigh around,
That I could think there trembled through
   His happy good-night air
Some blessed Hope, whereof he knew
   And I was unaware.

Thomas Hardy

Thrushes

Terrifying are the attent sleek thrushes on the lawn,
More coiled steel than living – a poised
Dark deadly eye, those delicate legs
Triggered to stirrings beyond sense – with a start, a bounce, a stab
Overtake the instant and drag out some writhing thing.
No indolent procrastinations and no yawning stares.
No sighs or head-scratchings. Nothing but bounce and stab
And a ravening second.

Is it their single-minded-sized skulls, or a trained
Body, or genius, or a nestful of brats
Gives their days this bullet and automatic
Purpose? Mozart's brain had it, and the shark's mouth
That hungers down the blood-smell even to a leak of its own
Side and devouring of itself: efficiency which
Strikes too streamlined for any doubt to pluck at it
Or obstruction deflect.

With a man it is otherwise. Heroisms on horseback,
Outstripping his desk-diary at a broad desk,
Carving at a tiny ivory ornament
For years: his act worships itself – while for him,
Though he bends to be blent in the prayer, how loud and above what
Furious spaces of fire do the distracting devils

Orgy and hosannah, under what wilderness
Of black silent waters weep.

Ted Hughes

ACTIVITY
1 Make detailed notes on the language, imagery and ideas in each of the three poems.
2 Think about what each poet has to say about the relationship between human beings and the natural world, as represented by the thrushes. How may this relate to the different times at which they were written? Look at the introductory paragraphs for this unit for some ideas about how views of nature have changed over time.
3 If you are working as a group, you could divide the poems among individuals or pairs, make notes and present your findings to each other before going on to discuss the similarities and differences between them.
4 Choose two, or all three, of the poems and write a detailed critical comparison of how the poets reveal their attitudes to nature through their reflections on the thrushes.

Student response

David has chosen to write about the poems by Hardy and Hughes. When you have completed your own answer, read his response and compare it with yours. Are there any useful points he has made that you have missed, or vice versa? Does he express himself clearly? What are the strengths of his work? What could he improve? What about your own performance?

> The two poems, 'Thrushes' by Ted Hughes, and 'The Darkling Thrush' by Thomas Hardy convey to the reader two very different perspectives of the birds. This reveals a lot about the poets' attitudes to nature.
>
> 'Thrushes' begins with a detailed description of the thrushes. After altering the syntax of the sentence to place emphasis on the adjective 'terrifying', the poet describes the birds as 'attent' and 'sleek'. All of this description comes before it is mentioned that they are thrushes. This is immediately striking to the reader, who would not usually attach the connotations we get from these adjectives to such an animal. In comparison, Hardy begins his poem by focusing on the general atmosphere of the last day of the century. The sense of a bleak, miserable day is conveyed through the adjective 'desolate', whilst 'Winter's dregs' has connotations of the wet and muddy days after snow. An eerie, almost supernatural atmosphere is depicted through 'spectre gray' and the verb 'haunted' in conjunction with 'all mankind'. This conveys to the reader that Hardy feels isolated and lonely in this landscape.
>
> Hughes continues in the first poem by using a metaphor of a machine to describe the thrushes. 'Coiled steel' and the adjective 'poised' depicts how the thrush waits for 'stirrings beyond sense'. This description of animal instinct is made sinister by the adjectives 'dark' and 'deadly'. 'The Darkling

Thrush' also becomes more sinister as Hardy uses the metaphor of a 'corpse' in place of the end of the century. The nouns 'crypt' and 'spirit' continue the supernatural and morbid theme. Following on from the unusual musical simile 'broken lyres' of the first verse, is 'death lament'. Conventionally music is used to symbolize joy, though here Hardy uses it to express his depression.

As though describing Hardy's poem, Hughes uses the human characteristics of 'indolent procrastination' and 'head-scratchings' to contrast the instinct of his thrushes with human behaviour. Hardy encapsulates these characteristics when he labels himself 'fervourless'.

Hughes decides that the thrushes are either 'single-minded', 'genius' or are motivated by parental instincts to feed their 'nestful of brats'. The thrushes are then compared to an animal that is much more synonymous with danger and death: a 'shark'. The verb 'devouring' is in no way dissimilar to the 'ravening' of the thrushes. An equally unusual comparison is to 'Mozart', whose own 'single-minded-sized skull' was focused on music. Hardy's thrush is a contrast to Hughes's, as it is 'frail, gaunt and small' in appearance. 'Blast-beruffled plume' is a contrast to 'sleek'. Continuing the theme of music is 'full-hearted evensong' which brings a change in tone for the poem. The thrush is then contrasted to Hardy himself, as it has enthusiasm enough to 'fling his soul' into a song. This has connotations of extreme enthusiasm or, as it is his 'soul', religious fervour.

Hughes also contrasts the thrushes' instinct to humans. Whilst a thrush can take a 'second' on its business of catching a worm, humans can take 'years' over imaginary 'heroisms on horseback' or 'carving at a tiny ornament'. Whilst 'Thrushes' ends on a sinister and almost evil tone, with 'devils' Orgy', 'The Darkling Thrush' is light and almost happy in tone as Hardy now feels 'some blessed Hope'.

David

Examiner's comments

- This question asks you to do two things, which are inter-related: to compare the poems in detail and in so doing, to explore each poet's attitude to nature. This means that you need to demonstrate skill in close reading and analysis and also to give an overview of the ideas expressed in each poem.
- David tackles the first of these requirements admirably. He pays attention to details of language, thinking carefully about the effect and 'connotations' or associations of particular words and phrases – for example, where he explores the language Hardy uses to create atmosphere on 'the last day of the century', and makes some effective comparisons between details in the poems.
- He deals with the 'overview' less effectively. He obviously has an understanding of the ideas in the poems, which relate the birds to

humans in very different ways, but he tends to imply this in his analysis, rather than making it clear and explicit. He could improve this by including a summary or explanation of the poets' central concerns, either just after his opening paragraph, which introduces the idea that the 'different perspectives of the birds reveals a lot about the poets' attitudes to nature', or later in his essay, to give it a stronger conclusion. Though it is not expected here, some similar questions might also require you to demonstrate your awareness of context, by asking you to relate the poems to an understanding of the ways attitudes to nature have changed over time.

- David's written style is clear and his short quotations are well-chosen and neatly integrated into his writing. He needs to keep the main thrust of the question in mind so that he sees the wood as well as the trees.

Student response

Now compare this response, by Olwen, which has different qualities. Discuss its strengths and write down some suggestions for improving it.

As the titles suggest, 'Thrushes' and 'The Darkling Thrush' are both about the birds of that name. However, each poem creates a completely different outlook on life through focusing on the lives of this bird in completely different ways.

'The Darkling Thrush' by Thomas Hardy has a depressive tone which is reflected through the choice of language, phrases such as 'Spectre-gray', and 'Winter's dregs' create dark and blackened images. The use of capital letters on 'Frost' and 'Winter' convey a sense of overwhelming power over the 'desolate' sun. Hardy's use of the verb 'haunted' suggests that the people around him seem ghost-like because he is lonely and so he can't connect to the human or the natural environment.

In contrast, 'Thrushes', by Ted Hughes has a more upbeat tone. The disrupted syntax of the opening line creates dramatic emphasis on the word 'Terrifying', and the fact that it is the 'thrushes' who are supposedly terrifying creates an element of surprise.

Both Hardy's and Hughes' thrushes are alert but for different purposes which creates a contrasting view of nature. Hughes suggests that the thrush is alive and waiting to kill because of its animal instincts, it has 'Stirrings beyond sense', because this is its purpose in life. In contrast, Hardy uses anthropomorphism and suggests that the bird is alive to sing in praise of God, he does this by surrounding the thrush with religious language as he describes its 'evensong'.

When Hardy hears the thrush's song in 'The Darkling Thrush' there is a change of tone in the poem which is reflected in the structure of the poem as the rhythm becomes very definite in the line, 'At once a voice arose *among.' The lack of punctuation mirrors how the bird's song flows. However, Hardy then uses punctuation to draw the reader's attention to the words, 'Frail, gaunt, and small'. It almost comes as a surprise that a bird singing with such 'joy' is small and old and so Hardy conveys his own surprise. Hughes uses punctuation in 'Thrushes', to describe the sporadic movement of the thrush. The use of commas in between 'A start, a bounce, a stab,' breaks the rhythm of the line and reflects the movement of the thrush.*

Both Hardy and Hughes are somewhat in awe of the thrush though for different reasons. Hardy's thrush gives him 'Hope', because if an old, fragile bird has a reason to sing, 'full-hearted' then he himself has to have faith. The bird's song gives him hope in the 'growing gloom.' The alliteration in this phrase makes it hard to say if Hardy deliberately did this to draw our attention to the phrase as it provides a contrast to the vitality of the bird. In contrast Hughes is in awe of the 'attent, sleek' thrush who uses and works with his environment. Hughes is almost criticizing Hardy when he says that a thrush has 'No indolent procrastinations and no yawning stares,' because Hardy himself is guilty of this. The message of Hughes' poem becomes explicit when he states, 'With a man it is otherwise.' The thrush is programmed from birth to do what it does and so it kills on instinct. Hughes forces humans to look at their own intellectual capacity.

The bird in Hardy's 'The Darkling Thrush' forces him to look at nature in a new light instead of dwelling on what might have been. in contrast, Hughes is in awe of nature's own 'killing machines' and is forced to look at his own life instead.

Olwen

Some people choose to challenge themselves by exploring the natural world at its most extreme. The world's wildest landscapes seem to make people particularly sensitive to the mysteries of existence and the fragility of life, and furnish writers with metaphors for human emotion and experience. The extracts which follow are by two contemporary writers who made journeys which were in some way quests for meaning or greater understanding.

In *Skating to Antarctica*, Jenny Diski combines travel writing with an exploration of her own past. Following an urge to find complete 'whiteness' and to reach a better understanding of herself and her own depression, she took the unusual step of visiting Antarctica. Peter Matthiessen, a more experienced traveller, went trekking in a remote area of the Himalayas in the hope of catching a glimpse of the rare and elusive snow leopard. Where Diski is concerned with making sense of the past, Matthiessen's writing reflects his interest in Buddhist meditation, through which he aims to gain a clearer sense of himself and his own nature in the present moment.

Skating to Antarctica

As we approached the slightly protected bay, the wind let up a little and it was possible to look up, straight ahead towards the land. We were being watched. The long shoreline and the beach right back to the glacier and mountains were packed so tight with penguins that they formed a continuous carpet. A legion of black faces and orange beaks pointed out to sea facing in our direction, seeming to observe our arrival. St Andrew's Bay is famously the breeding ground for 100,000 king penguins (I don't know who counted but I'm not inclined to argue), and there they all were, standing in serried ranks, watching without curiosity as half a dozen black rubber dinghies came towards them. To us, they did seem to be watching, but then again, quantum physics notwithstanding, if we hadn't been approaching the shore, if the sea had been deserted, they would still all be standing there looking out to sea. That's what penguins do. Stand. Every year, for thousands of years, for hundreds of thousands of years for all I know, 100,000 penguins stand along this beach, mating and incubating eggs. One day, once a year or so, black rubber dinghies approach, and a handful of people come to the bay, believing that the penguins are watching them arrive. For the penguins, it's just another day of standing and staring. They were not even slightly interested at our approach. We made a wet landing in knee-deep icy water and clambered up on to the rocky land. The penguins parted slightly to make way for us, but they still stood looking out to sea. The fact is that on land the only thing a penguin has to fear are the swooping skuas, diving through the air for their eggs and chicks. Danger comes from above, not from the sea or the land. It seemed that they didn't even compute humans and their noisy boats. We were not part of their existence, presented no obvious danger and therefore were ignored, quite overlooked. You could walk right up to them and they would take no notice. If you stood in their way as they waddled along their track from nest to sea to feed, they stopped a few inches from your feet and made a small, semicircular detour around you, as they would if they found a boulder in their way. If you got down on your knees and faced them eyeball to eyeball, they looked back, turning an eye towards you, but deciding what you were not, lost interest rapidly.

I was very taken with this timeless standing, unwitnessed, unwitnessing, that we were interrupting, though only barely. That was the point, for me, of Antarctica; that it was simply there, always had been, always would be, with great tracts of the continent unseen, unwitnessed, cycling through its two seasons, the ice rolling slowly from the centre to the edges where eventually it breaks off. A place that is and always has been unseen. Now these penguins, getting on with what they do, standing in their place. And on this or that day, a group of people arrive for a visit and make not the slightest difference to anything at all. South Georgia is so out of the way that fewer people visit it than the Antarctic mainland. Only a couple of hundred people a year arrived at Grytviken, fewer still, I imagine, land at St Andrew's Bay. I ached for the endurance and the indifference of this landscape and its penguin inhabitants.

My fellow travellers were filming and photographing up a storm. The word 'cute' was heard for the first time, but multiplied like an echo. Penguins, in fact, are cute. They have a ridiculous dignity to our eyes: upstanding, busy creatures, who are hopelessly designed for life on land, but seem determined to overcome their disability. They waddle furiously about their business, marching in orderly lines along set tracks down to the sea to get food for themselves and their mates. But every now and again they drop the front, as we might if we thought we were alone and unobserved, and finding it tedious walking down an incline, take to their bellies and slide down the slippery slope. Poised between fake dignity and letting their hair down, they seem remarkably like caricatures of ourselves. So they make us laugh, as children do. Penguins, you can be sure, don't see things this way, but quantum physics withstanding this time, it's us doing the looking. It's impossible not to be anthropomorphic, and I'm not sure why we should try. I don't really believe that the penguins are damaged by our self-centred view of them, providing they are left alone to get on with their lives. Relating the natural world to ourselves is what we do, just as standing staring out to sea is what penguins do.

However, it was fairly clear that penguin life is not that cute. The skuas wheeled overhead waiting for an opportunity to take what they could. And the standing and staring became on close inspection a frantic business. The colony was full of fevered activity. Lines of penguins marched back and forth to the shore, up and down impossibly steep inclines, in order to provide for their mates and their offspring. Once in the sea they are vulnerable to seals. On land, if a mate doesn't return from foraging, the brooding penguin and its hard-worked-for egg will die of starvation. In the middle of the beach, as I began to walk along it, there was an empty space in the centre of which a penguin stood perfectly still, while eighteen inches away a large grey and white skua sat with monumental patience. They ignored each other, at least in the sense that neither looked at or took notice of the other. It seemed charming, two creatures at ease with each other, veritable lion laying down with the lamb stuff, until I got closer and saw a great florid gash running down the penguin's side. The skua was waiting for the penguin's final, inevitable collapse, to provide it and its young with an easy and very substantial meal. To be entirely anthropomorphic about it, the sight was heartbreaking. It's not much of a life being a penguin.

Jenny Diski

The Snow Leopard

November 11

At daybreak, when the blue-black turns to silver in the east, the moon sets with the darkness in the west. On frozen sun rays, fourteen pigeons come to pick about the yard, pale blue-grey birds with a broad white band across the tail that fills with light as they flutter down upon the rigid walls. Like all wild things at Crystal Mountain, the hill pigeons are tame, and do not fly as I draw near, but cock their gentle dovelike heads to see me better.

I climb the mountain with the sun, and find the mixed herd high up on the slope; I try angling toward them, then away again, zig-zagging as I climb. For some reason, this seems to reassure them, for after watching me awhile, and perhaps concluding that I am not to be taken seriously, they go on about their business, which this morning is unusually dull. I keep on climbing. Far below, the torrent, freed from daybreak ice, carries grey scree down out of the mountains.

In hope of seeing the snow leopard, I have made a wind shelter and lookout on this mountain, just at snow line, that faces north over the Black Canyon all the way to the pale terraces below Samling. From here, the Tsakang mountainsides across Black River are in view, and the cliff caves too, and the slopes between ravines, so that most of the blue sheep in this region may be seen should they be set upon by wolf or leopard. . . . Unlike the wolves, the leopard cannot eat everything at once, and may remain in the vicinity of its kill for several days. Therefore our best hope is to see the griffons gather, and the choughs and ravens, and the lammergeier.

The Himalayan griffon, buff and brown, is almost the size of the great lammergeier; its graceful turns against the peaks inspire the Tibetans, who like the vanished Aryans of the Vedas, revere the wind and sky. Blue and white are the celestial colours of the B'on sky god, who is seen as an embodiment of space and light, and creatures of the upper air become B'on symbols – the griffon, the mythical garuda, and the dragon. For Buddhist Tibetans, prayer flags and wind-bells confide spiritual longings to the winds, and the red kites that dance on holidays over the old brown city of Kathmandu are of Tibetan origin as well. There is also a custom called 'air burial', in which the body of the deceased is set out on a wild crag such as this one, to be rended and devoured by the wild beasts; when only the bones are left, these are broken and ground down to powder, then mixed into lumps of dough, to be set out again for passing birds. Thus all is returned into the elements, death into life.

Against the faces of the canyon, shadows of griffons turn. Perhaps the Somdo raptors think that this queer lump on the landscape – the motionless form of a man in meditation – is the defunct celebrant in an air-burial, for a young eagle, plumage burnished a heraldic bronzy-black, draws near with its high peeping, and a lammergeier, approaching from behind, descends with a sudden rush of feathers, sweeping so close past my head that I feel the break of air. This whisper of the shroud gives me a start, and my sudden jump flares the dark bird, causing it to take four deep strokes – the only movement of the wings that I was ever to observe in this great sailer that sweeps up and down the Himalayan canyons, the cold air ringing in its golden head.

Dark, light, dark: a raptor, scimitar-winged, under the sun peak – I know, I know. In such a light, one might hope to see the shadow of that bird upon the sky.

The ground whirls with its own energy, not in an alarming way but in slow spiral, and at these altitudes, in this vast space and silence, that energy pours through me, joining my body with the sun until small silver breaths of cold, clear air, no longer mine, are lost in the mineral breathing of the mountain. A white down feather, sun-filled, dances before me on the wind: alighting nowhere, it balances on a shining thorn, goes spinning on. Between this white feather, sheep dung, light, and the fleeting aggregate of atoms that is 'I', there is no particle of difference. There is a mountain opposite, but this 'I' is opposite nothing, opposed to nothing.

Peter Matthiessen

ACTIVITY

1 Both writers observe birds in their natural habitats. Make notes on the ways in which they use language and imagery in their descriptions of the birds and how each writer reflects on their behaviour.

2 How do these two writers approach the natural world? Where do they place themselves in the picture – inside or outside? What ideas does each suggest about the relationship between human life and nature? How is this reflected in their writing? Discuss the similarities and differences between them.

3 Write a detailed comparison of the content and language of extracts H and I, exploring the ways in which each writer responds to the natural world.

'Nature, Red in Tooth and Claw'?

Further activities

1 Choosing two extracts as a starting point, examine some of the different ways in which writers of different eras explore the significance of nature. Refer also to your own wider reading, if it is relevant.

2 Is nature a comfort or a threat? Compare and contrast the attitudes to nature shown by the writers of at least three of the extracts in this unit.

3 Where do writers place themselves, as human beings, in relation to the natural world – as insider or outsiders? How do they reveal this in the extracts here or in other texts you have studied? Write in detail on at least two texts.

2

Satirical Voices

Most authors write about the society in which they live, and often they find plenty to criticize. Not surprisingly, they sometimes choose to satirize or 'send up' the foolishness of society's customs, beliefs or politics. Satirists may mock trivial things, such as the foibles, weaknesses or hypocrisies of individuals; but often they make wider points, angrily using their wit to attack cruelty or injustice, in the hope that they might shock or move people into making changes.

Whether they are writing gentle mockery or fierce and bitter criticism, satirists are likely to use a variety of techniques, such as:

- **irony**, where the writer appears to say one thing on the surface, but means something different, perhaps even the opposite;
- **sarcasm**, which is usually spoken, expresses scorn or contempt and may also involve irony, but relies more on tone of voice to convey the speaker's intentions;
- **invective** – more directly abusive or attacking language;
- other forms of **wit** – jokes and wordplay, for example;
- **exaggeration** of something real to draw out its ridiculous aspects;
- inventing a **parallel** situation or society, which can be used to mock the real target;
- creating a **persona** and writing in a different voice; this enables the writer to mock the type of person or attitude represented, as well as making other points.

In England, a great deal of powerful satirical writing was produced in the late seventeenth and early eighteenth centuries, after the restoration of the monarchy and during the reign of Queen Anne. This period is known as the **Augustan** era, because writers of that time had a high regard for the classical literature of Ancient Greece and Rome, likening their own age to the age of the Emperor Augustus in Rome, when Latin poetry was particularly impressive. Much of their work was in the **heroic couplets** (rhymed couplets of iambic pentameter) favoured by the Romans.

Three of the most important Augustan writers were:

John Dryden (1631–1700)
Alexander Pope (1688–1744)
Jonathan Swift (1667–1745)

All three used satire to draw attention in particular to hypocrisy and artificiality, showing up people or aspects of society that were not what they seemed. In the centuries since then, writers have continued to use satire – Dickens is frequently satirical in his novels, for example. However, it has tended to be less overt and central, until recent times. Today, satirists have a much wider range of media to work with. As well as satirical writing, they can use television, radio and film to mock and criticize. This leads us to an important question about satire: since it often tends to be concerned with the politics or habits or people of a particular time, to what extent will it interest readers or audiences of future generations? Is it of lasting value, or is it merely ephemeral? It seems that satire which is too personal and specific to its time may lose its appeal quite quickly, but if it targets universal situations or aspects of human nature, there is a greater chance that it will hold our interest. This is something to bear in mind as you read the texts that follow.

An Essay upon Satire

Here, Dryden and 'Mulgrave' (Sheffield, Duke of Buckingham) give their definition of satire in the opening lines of their 'essay' on the subject, written in 1679.

How dull, and how insensible a beast
Is man, who yet would lord it o'er the rest!
Philosophers and poets vainly strove
In every age the lumpish mass to move:
But those were pedants, when compared with these,
Who know not only to instruct, but please.
Poets alone found the delightful way,
Mysterious morals gently to convey
In charming numbers: so that as men grew
Pleased with their poems, they grew wiser too.
Satire has always shone among the rest,
And is the boldest way, if not the best,
To tell men freely of their foulest faults;
To laugh at their vain deeds, and vainer thoughts.
In satire too the wise took different ways,
To each deserving its peculiar praise.
Some did all folly with just sharpness blame,
Whilst others laugh'd and scorn'd them into shame.
But of these two, the last succeeded best,
As men aim rightest when they shoot in jest.

Dryden and the Earl of Mulgrave

ACTIVITY

1　What are the purposes and characteristics of satire, according to Dryden and Mulgrave? Underline or note what you think are the key words and phrases in the extract.

2　Why has satire 'shone among the rest'? Write a few paragraphs explaining these ideas in your own words.

The Rape of the Lock

In this 'Heroi-Comical' poem of 1712, Alexander Pope writes a relatively gentle satire on the vanities of court life, 'intended only', he tells us in the dedication, 'to divert a few young ladies, who have good sense and good humour enough to laugh not only at their sex's little unguarded follies, but at their own'. The 'plot' of the poem concerns the theft, by one of her admirers, of a girl's lock of hair, a story told with much comic exaggeration, using the language of the classical **pastoral** world of nymphs and shepherds. Here, Queen Anne's courtiers gather to drink tea and play cards at Hampton Court Palace. Notice Pope's humorous use of **bathos**, where his high-flown language suddenly comes down to earth with a bump.

Close by those meads, for ever crowned with flowers,
Where Thames with pride surveys his rising towers,
There stands a structure of majestic frame,
Which from the neighbouring Hampton takes its name.
Here Britain's statesmen oft the fall foredoom
Of foreign tyrants, and of nymphs at home;
Here thou, great ANNA! whom three realms obey,
Dost sometimes counsel take – and sometimes tea.
　Hither the heroes and the nymphs resort,
To taste awhile the pleasures of a court;
In various talk th'instructive hours they passed,
Who gave the ball, or paid the visit last:
One speaks the glory of the British Queen
And one describes a charming Indian screen;
A third interprets motions, looks, and eyes;
At every word a reputation dies.
Snuff, or the fan, supply each pause of chat,
With singing, laughing, ogling, and all that.
　Meanwhile, declining from the noon of day,
The sun obliquely shoots his burning ray;
The hungry judges soon the sentence sign,
And wretches hang that jurymen may dine;
The merchant from th'Exchange returns in peace,
And the long labours of the toilet cease.

Alexander Pope

ACTIVITY

1 Make notes on Pope's use of language, including examples of pastoral, comic exaggeration, and bathos.
2 Write a detailed commentary on the extract, focusing on how language is used to mock and create humour, and pointing out ways in which it matches Dryden's definition of satire in extract A.

Dombey and Son

Charles Dickens regularly used a satirical voice to criticize aspects of life in Victorian England. He was particularly conscious of the wide difference between the lives of people of different social classes, and also of the ways in which people could be failed by the institutions that were supposed to benefit them. Here, we are introduced to Doctor Blimber's school, where little Paul Dombey is about to become a pupil.

Whenever a young gentleman was taken in hand by Doctor Blimber, he might consider himself sure of a pretty tight squeeze. The Doctor only undertook the charge of ten young gentlemen, but he had, always ready, a supply of learning for a hundred, on the lowest estimate; and it was at once the business and delight of his life to gorge the unhappy ten with it.

In fact, Doctor Blimber's establishment was a great hot-house, in which there was a forcing apparatus incessantly at work. All the boys blew before their time. Mental green-peas were produced at Christmas, and intellectual asparagus all the year round. Mathematical gooseberries (very sour ones too) were common at untimely seasons, and from mere sprouts of bushes, under Doctor Blimber's cultivation. Every description of Greek and Latin vegetable was got off the driest twigs of boys, under the frostiest circumstances. Nature was of no consequence at all. No matter what a young gentleman was intended to bear, Doctor Blimber made him bear to pattern, somehow or other.

This was all very pleasant and ingenious, but the system of forcing was attended with its usual disadvantages. There was not the right taste about the premature productions, and they didn't keep well. Moreover, one young gentleman, with a swollen nose and an excessively large head (the oldest of the ten who had 'gone through' everything), suddenly left off blowing one day, and remained in the establishment a mere stalk. And people did say that the Doctor had rather overdone it with young Toots, and that when he began to have whiskers he left off having brains.

There young Toots was, at any rate; possessed of the gruffest of voices and the shrillest of minds; sticking ornamental pins into his shirt, and keeping a ring in his waistcoat pocket to put on his little finger by stealth, when the pupils went out walking; constantly falling in love by sight with nursery-maids, who had no idea of his existence; and looking at the gas-lighted world over the little iron bars in the left-hand corner window of the front three pairs of stairs, after bed-time, like a greatly overgrown cherub who had sat up aloft much too long.

The Doctor was a portly gentleman in a suit of black, with strings at his knees, and stockings below them. He had a bald head, highly polished; a deep voice; and a chin so very double, that it was a wonder how he ever managed to shave into the creases. He had likewise a pair of little eyes that were always half shut up, and a mouth that was always half-expanded into a grin, as if he had, that moment, posed a boy, and were waiting to convict him from his own lips. Insomuch, that when the Doctor put his right hand into the breast of his coat, and with his other hand behind him, and a scarcely perceptible wag of his head, made the commonest observation to a nervous stranger, it was like a sentiment from the Sphinx, and settled his business. . . .

As to Mr Feeder, B.A., Doctor Blimber's assistant, he was a kind of human barrel-organ, with a little list of tunes at which he was continually working, over and over again, without any variation. He might have been fitted up with a change of barrels, perhaps, in early life, if his destiny had been favourable; but it had not been; and he had only one, with which, in a monotonous round, it was his occupation to bewilder the young ideas of Doctor Blimber's young gentlemen. The young gentlemen were prematurely full of carking anxieties. They knew no rest from the pursuit of stony-hearted verbs, savage noun-substantives, inflexible syntactic passages, and ghosts of exercises that appeared to them in their dreams. Under the forcing system, a young gentleman usually took leave of his spirits in three weeks. He had all the cares of the world on his head in three months. He conceived bitter sentiments against his parents or guardians in four; he was an old misanthrope, in five; . . . and at the end of the first twelvemonth had arrived at the conclusion, from which he never afterwards departed, that all the fancies of the poets, and lessons of the sages, were a mere collection of words and grammar, and had no other meaning in the world.

But he went on, blow, blow, blowing, in the Doctor's hothouse, all the time; and the Doctor's glory and reputation were great, when he took his wintry growth home to his relations and friends.

Charles Dickens

ACTIVITY
1 Discuss and make notes on the language and imagery Dickens uses to mock Doctor Blimber's school.
2 Write a close study of the passage, considering it as an example of satire. Refer to other texts included here or to your own reading if you wish.

Gulliver's Travels

Swift's *Gulliver's Travels*, published in 1726, is one of the best known satirical texts of all time. You are probably familiar with the tale of Gulliver's voyage to Lilliput, which is often read as a childrens' story, but which is only the first of four sections of a large-scale, biting satire on many aspects of life in the early eighteenth century. Accounts of 'journeys', sometimes real, sometimes imaginary, were fashionable at the time. Swift recounts these 'voyages' through the persona of Gulliver, a ship's surgeon turned sea-captain. This enables him to mock Gulliver's attitudes as well as what he actually describes.

This extract is from Gulliver's fourth voyage, in which he finds himself in the land of the Houyhnhnms, a society in which horses are very civilized, reasonable beings, while Yahoos, the nearest equivalent to humans, are vile and brutish. At first, Gulliver is keen to educate the Houyhnhnms about human society, but the longer he stays with them, the more he recognizes the negative aspects of human nature. Swift was criticized for being *too* cynical in this voyage, but he said himself that he hoped *Gulliver's Travels* would 'vex the world rather than divert it'. Here, Gulliver tries to explain war to his Houyhnhnm master.

He asked me what were the usual causes or motives that made one country go to war with another. I answered they were innumerable, but I should only mention a few of the chief. Sometimes the ambition of princes, who never think they have land or people enough to govern: sometimes the corruption of ministers, who engage their master in a war in order to stifle or divert the clamour of the subjects against their evil administration. Differences in opinions hath cost many millions of lives: for instance, whether *flesh* be *bread*, or *bread* be *flesh*; whether the juice of a certain *berry* be *blood* or *wine*; whether *whistling* be a vice or a virtue; whether it be better to *kiss a post*, or throw it into the fire; what is the best colour for a *coat*, whether *black*, *white*, *red* or *grey*; and whether it should be *long* or *short*, *narrow* or *wide*, *dirty* or *clean*, with many more. Neither are any wars so furious and bloody, or of so long continuance, as those occasioned by difference in opinion, especially if it be in things indifferent.

Sometimes the quarrel between two princes is to decide which of them shall dispossess a third of his dominions, where neither of them pretend to any right. Sometimes one prince quarelleth with another, for fear the other should quarrel with him. Sometimes a war is entered upon, because the enemy is too *strong*, and sometimes because he is too *weak*. Sometimes our neighbours *want* the *things* which we *have*, or *have* the *things* which we *want*; and we both fight, till they take ours or give us theirs. It is a very justifiable cause of war to invade a country after the people have been wasted by famine, destroyed by pestilence, or embroiled by factions amongst themselves. It is justifiable to enter into a war against our nearest ally, when one of his towns lies convenient for us, or a territory of land, that would render our dominions round and compact. If a prince send forces into a nation where the people are poor and ignorant, he may lawfully put half of them to death, and make slaves of the rest, in order to civilize and reduce them from their barbarous way of living. It is a very kingly, honourable, and frequent practice, when one prince desires the assistance of another to secure him against an invasion, that the assistant, when he hath driven out the invader, should seize on the dominions himself, and kill, imprison or banish the prince he came to relieve. Alliance by blood or marriage is a sufficient cause of war between princes, and the nearer the kindred is, the greater is their disposition to quarrel: *poor* nations are *hungry*, and *rich* nations are *proud*, and *pride* and *hunger* will ever be at variance. For these reasons, the trade of a *soldier* is held the most honourable of all others: because a *soldier* is a Yahoo hired to kill in cold blood as many of his own species, who have never offended him, as possibly he can.

There is likewise a kind of beggarly princes in Europe, not able to make war themselves, who hire out their troops to richer nations, for so much a day to each man; of which they keep three fourths to themselves, and it is the best part of their maintenance; such are those in Germany and northern parts of Europe.

What you have told me (said my master), upon the subject of war, doth indeed discover most admirably the effects of that Reason you pretend to: however, it is happy that the *shame* is greater than the *danger*; and that Nature hath left you utterly incapable of doing much mischief. For your mouths lying flat with your faces, you can hardly bite each other to any purpose, unless by consent. Then as to the claws upon your feet before and behind, they are so short and tender, that one of our Yahoos would drive a dozen of yours before him. And therefore in recounting the numbers of those who have been killed in battle, I cannot but think that you have *said the thing which is not.*

I could not forbear shaking my head and smiling a little at his ignorance. And, being no stranger to the art of war, I gave him a description of cannons, culverins, muskets, carabines, pistols, bullets, powder, swords, bayonets, battles, sieges, retreats, attacks, undermines, countermines, bombardments, sea-fights; ships sunk with a thousand men, twenty thousand killed on each side; dying groans, limbs flying in the air, smoke, noise, confusion, trampling to death under horses' feet; flight, pursuit, victory; fields strewed with carcasses left for food to dogs, and wolves, and birds of prey; plundering, stripping, ravishing, burning, and destroying. And to set forth the valour of my own dear countrymen, I assured him, that I had seen them blow up a hundred enemies at once in a siege, and as many in a ship, and beheld the dead bodies drop down in pieces from the clouds, to the great diversion of all the spectators.

I was going on to more particulars, when my master commanded me silence. He said, whoever understood the nature of Yahoos might easily believe it possible for so vile an animal to be capable of every action I had named, if their strength and cunning equalled their malice. But as my discourse had increased his abhorrence of the whole species, so he found it gave him a disturbance in his mind, to which he was wholly a stranger before. He thought his ears being used to such abominable words, might by degrees admit them with less detestation. That although he hated the Yahoos of this country, yet he no more blamed them for their odious qualities than he did a *gnnayh* (a bird of prey) for its cruelty, or a sharp stone for cutting his hoof. But when a creature pretending to Reason could be capable of such enormities, he dreaded lest the corruption of that faculty might be worse than brutality itself. He seemed therefore confident, that instead of Reason, we were only possessed of some quality fitted to increase our natural vices; as the reflection from a troubled stream returns the image of an ill-shapen body, not only *larger*, but more *distorted*.

Jonathan Swift

ACTIVITY

1 What qualities are suggested by Gulliver's name? How does Swift present – and undermine – Gulliver as a narrator? Note as many examples as you can where Swift 'gives him away'.
2 Write a commentary on the extract, exploring the extent to which Swift is likely to 'vex' his readers, rather than 'divert' them.

Oh What a Lovely War

Oh What a Lovely War, first staged in 1963, is a musical show or revue, which satirically depicts the First World War. It is to be performed by a troop of *pierrots*, or live 'puppets', and makes use of songs, dance, and projector slides, as well as dialogue and acting. This extract is taken from near the end of the show – and of the war, when the long stalemate of trench warfare was about to be ended by the arrival of American troops. Various members of the cast are on 'Sunday parade'.

Oh What a Lovely War *successfully satirized the tragedy of the First World War*

Act II

Chaplain: Let us pray. O God, show thy face to us as thou didst with thy angel at Mons. The choir will now sing 'What a friend we have in Jesus' as we offer a silent prayer for Sir Douglas Haig for success in tomorrow's onset.

SONG   WHEN THIS LOUSY WAR IS OVER
                        (*Tune: 'What a friend we have in Jesus'*)

When this lousy war is over,
No more soldiering for me,
Oh, how happy I shall be!
No more church parades on Sunday,
No more putting in for leave,
I shall kiss the sergeant-major,
How I'll miss him, how he'll grieve!
Amen.

Chaplain: O Lord, now lettest thou thy servant depart in peace, according to
thy word. Dismiss.
Corporal: (*blowing a whistle*) Come on, you men, fall in.

(*The soldiers sing as they march off.*)

SONG   WASH ME IN THE WATER

Whiter than the whitewash on the wall,
Whiter than the whitewash on the wall,
Oh, wash me in the water that you wash your dirty daughter in,
And I shall be whiter than the whitewash on the wall,
On the wall . . .

Chaplain: Land of our birth, we pledge to thee, our love and toil in the years
to be.
Haig: Well, God, the prospects for a successful attack are now ideal. I place
myself in thy hands.
Chaplain: Into thy hands I commend my spirit.
Nurse: The fields are full of tents, O Lord, all empty except for as yet unmade
and naked iron bedsteads. Every ward has been cleared to make way for
the wounded that will be arriving when the big push comes.
Haig: I trust you will understand, Lord, that as a British gentleman I could not
subordinate myself to the ambitions of a junior foreign commander as the
politicians suggested. It is for the prestige of my King and Empire, Lord.
Chaplain: Teach us to rule ourself always, controlled and cleanly night and day.
Haig: I ask thee for victory, Lord, before the Americans arrive.
Nurse: The doctors say there will be enormous numbers of dead and
wounded, God.
Chaplain: That we may bring if need arise, no maimed or worthless sacrifice.
Haig: Thus to grant us fair weather for tomorrow's attack, that we my drive
the enemy into the sea.
Nurse: O Lord, I beg you, do not let this dreadful war cause all the suffering
that we have prepared for. I know you will answer my prayer.

(*Explosion. They go off.*)

(*A sequence of slides is shown as soldiers' voices sing offstage.*)

Slide 42: A group of eight or nine Highland infantrymen, around a small camp fire.

Slide 43: Two captured wounded German infantrymen, both sitting, one nursing a badly wounded leg, the other sewing.

Slide 44: A lull in the fighting. A trench of Tommies 'at ease' – some smoking, others doing running repairs on their kit.

Slide 45: Three Tommies walking through a rain-soaked muddy field.

Slide 46: Two captured Germans between two Tommies. One of the Germans is being given a drink of water by one of the Tommies.

Slide 47: A group of Tommies, skylarking and obviously off-duty, with a damaged old horse-drawn coach, upon which they've chalked '10 Downing Street'.

SONG   I WANT TO GO HOME

[42] I want to go home, [43] I want to go home, [44]
I don't want to go in the trenches no more,
Where whizzbangs and shrapnel they whistle and roar. [45]
Take me over the sea, [46] where the alleyman can't get at me; [47]
Oh my, I don't want to die, I want to go home.

NEWSPANEL: BY NOV 1916 . . . TWO AND A HALF MILLION MEN KILLED ON WESTERN FRONT.

(*The screen goes up to reveal soldiers in gas capes doing burial squad duty in mime.* **[General] Haig** *is on one of the balconies.*)

Haig: I thank you, God; the attack is a great success. Fighting has been severe, but that was to be expected. There has been some delay along the Menin Road, but the ground is thick with enemy dead. First reports from the clearing stations state that our casualties are only some sixty thousand: mostly slight. The wounded are very cheery indeed.

(*The soldiers sing as they work.*)

SONG   THE BELLS OF HELL

The bells of hell go ting-a-ling-ling,
For you but not for me,
And the little devils how they sing-a-ling-a-ling,
For you but not for me.
Oh death, where is thy sting-a-ling-a-ling,
Oh grave, thy victory?
The bells of hell go ting-a-ling-a-ling
For you but not for me.

NEWSPANEL: APRIL 17 . . . AISNE . . . ALLIED LOSS 180,000 MEN . . . GAIN NIL.

(*The soldiers sing again, more gaily.* **Haig** *conducts them, wearing a pierrot hat, as they dance.*)

. . .

Haig: (*reading a letter*) From Snowball to Douglas. Water and mud are increasing and becoming horrible. The longer days when they come will be most welcome, especially to the officers, who say the conditions are impairing their efficiency. The other ranks don't seem to mind so much.

First Soldier: Look out – we're awash! Hey, give us a hand; he's going under.

Second Soldier: Cor – he's worse than old Fred.

Third Soldier: Here, whatever happened to old Fred?

Second Soldier: I dunno. Haven't seen him since his last cry for help.

Fourth Soldier: That's right; he got sucked under.

Third Soldier: Oh no, he went sick.

Fifth Soldier: No, he went under.

Third Soldier: He went sick.

Second Soldier: He got sucked under, mate.

Third Soldier: Well, I bet you a fag he went sick.

Second Soldier: Don't be daft. You can't go sick here. You've got to lose your lungs, your liver, your lights . . .

Sergeant: Watch it!

Theatre Workshop: Charles Chilton and the members of the original cast

ACTIVITY

1 In a group, discuss and/or experiment with ways of reading or presenting the play. Make notes on the satirical techniques used, and on ways in which attention might be drawn to these in performance.

2 In what ways might it be significant that the play is to be presented by a troupe of 'pierrots' – human puppets, or clowns?

3 Write about the extract, exploring the ways in which you might expect an audience to respond to the show.

A Cold Coming

Poet Tony Harrison often adopts a satirical approach to contemporary issues. In 1990, Saddam Hussein led Iraq in an invasion of Kuwait, threatening oil supplies to 'western' nations. The United States, supported by the British, retaliated with the sophisticated technology of Cruise and Scud missiles. This 'Gulf War' was controversial, as was the coverage it received in the tabloid press. Harrison's poem, *A Cold Coming*, from which this extract is taken, is a response to a particularly horrific photograph of an Iraqi soldier, killed at the wheel of his truck, which appeared in many newspapers.

> *'A cold coming we had of it.'*
> T. S. ELIOT
> *Journey of the Magi*

I saw the charred Iraqi lean
towards me from bomb-blasted screen,

his windscreen wiper like a pen
ready to write down thoughts for men,

his windscreen wiper like a quill
he's reaching for to make his will.

I saw the charred Iraqi lean
like someone made of Plasticine

as though he'd stopped to ask the way
and this is what I heard him say:

'Don't be afraid I've picked on you
for this exclusive interview.

Isn't it your sort of poet's task
to find words for this frightening mask?

If that gadget that you've got records
words from such scorched vocal chords,

press RECORD before some dog
devours me mid-monologue.'

So I held the shaking microphone
closer to the crumbling bone:

'I read the news of three wise men
who left their sperm in nitrogen,

three foes of ours, three wise Marines
with sample flasks and magazines,

three wise soldiers from Seattle
who banked their sperm before the battle.

Did No. 1 say: God be thanked
I've got my precious semen banked.

And No. 2: O praise the Lord
my last best shot is safely stored.

And No. 3: Praise be to God
I left my wife my frozen wad?

So if their fate was to be gassed
at least they thought their name would last,

and though cold corpses in Kuwait
they could by proxy procreate.

Excuse a skull half roast, half bone
for using such a scornful tone.

It may seem out of all proportion
but I wish I'd taken their precaution.

They seemed the masters of their fate
with wisely jarred ejaculate.

Was it a propaganda coup
to make us think they'd cracked death too,

disinformation to defeat us
with no post-mortem millilitres?

Symbolic billions in reserve
made me, for one, lose heart and nerve.

On Saddam's pay we can't afford
to go and get our semen stored.

Sad to say that such high tech's
uncommon here. We're stuck with sex.

If you can conjure up and stretch
your imagination (and not retch)

the image of me beside my wife
closely clasped creating life . . .

(I let the unfleshed skull unfold
a story I'd been already told,

and idly tried to calculate
the content of ejaculate:

the sperm in one ejaculation
equals the whole Iraqi nation

times, roughly, let's say, 12.5
though that .5's not now alive.

Let's say the sperms were an amount
so many times the body count,

2,500 times at least
(but let's wait till the death toll's released!)

Whichever way Death seems outflanked
by one tube of cold bloblings banked.

Poor bloblings, maybe you've been blessed
with, of all fates possible, the best

according to Sophocles i.e.
'the best of fates is not to be'

a philosophy that's maybe bleak
for any but an ancient Greek

but difficult these days to escape
when spoken to by such a shape.

When you see men brought to such states
who wouldn't want that 'best of fates'

or in the world of Cruise and Scud
not go kryonic if he could,

spared the normal human doom
of having made it through the womb?)

He heard my thoughts and stopped the spool:
'I never thought life futile, fool!

Though all Hell began to drop
I never wanted life to stop.

I was filled with such a yearning
to stay in life as I was burning,

such a longing to be beside
my wife in bed before I died,

and, most, to have engendered there
a child untouched by war's despair.

So press RECORD! I want to reach
the warring nations with my speech.

Don't look away! I know it's hard
to keep regarding one so charred,

so disfigured by unfriendly fire
and think it once burned with desire.

Though fire has flayed off half my features
they once were like my fellow creatures',

till some screen-gazing crop-haired boy
from Iowa or Illinois,

equipped by ingenious technophile
put paid to my paternal smile

and made the face you see today
an armature half-patched with clay,

an icon framed, a looking glass
for devotees of 'kicking ass',

a mirror that returns the gaze
of victors on their victory days

and in the end stares out the watcher
who ducks behind his headline: GOTCHA!

or behind the flag-bedecked page 1
of the true to bold-type-setting SUN!

Tony Harrison

ACTIVITY
1 Discuss the ideas and issues in Harrison's poem. The photograph which inspired it is horrific and shocking. What effect does the poem have on you?
2 Discuss and make notes on the language and form of the poem and the ways in which these contribute to its satirical effect.
3 Write a detailed critical commentary on this extract from the poem.

Satirical Voices:

Further activities

1 By what means do the satirists represented here 'tell man freely of his foulest faults'? Choose three extracts to write about in detail.
2 Writing on the work of Swift in 1752, John, Earl of Orrery suggests that:

True humour ought to be kept up with decency, and dignity, or it loses every tincture of entertainment. Descriptions that shock our delicacy cannot have the least good effect upon our minds. They offend us, and we fly precipitately from the sight. We cannot stay long enough to examine, whether wit, sense, or morality, may be couched under such odious appearances.

How far do you agree with his view? Referring in detail to at least two texts in this unit and to any other satirical material you have read, discuss the ways in which satirists use shock tactics to affect their readers.

3 Jonathan Swift wrote regretfully about the satire of his age:

Though the present age may understand well enough the little hints we give, the parallels we draw, and the characters we describe, yet this will all be lost the next.

Referring to a range of satirical texts you have read, write about the extent to which you feel this kind of writing suffers from being ephemeral – too much of its own time to be of lasting interest.

4 Choose an idea that amuses you, or an issue you feel strongly about, and experiment with some satirical writing of your own.

Student response

Below is Patricia's response to Question 2. Read her answer and compare it with your own. Discuss the extent to which you think she succeeds in her essay. Can you suggest any improvements she could make?

> *This statement by John, Earl of Orrery seems to make a sensible point. If we do not gain entertainment or at least some gratification from what we read we are unlikely to keep reading it and more particularly with reference to satire if a piece of writing shocks or offends us unreasonably we will simply reject it, including whatever point it is making. I want to compare two of the texts that refer to war, Tony Harrison's 'A Cold Coming' and the extract from Swift's 'Gulliver's Travels'.*

There are two significant differences between these texts. Harrison is referring to a specific conflict, the Gulf War, a topical issue when the poem was written and the most widely reported war in history; whereas Swift is talking about all wars – the very principle of war. The other significant difference is the use of a narrator. Harrison uses the voice of the dead Iraqui soldier talking to the 'I', the poet; Swift creates a type of discussion between Gulliver the human – like us – and his Houyhnhnm with apparently no authorial voice.

Both these texts aim to shock the reader but do so in different ways. Harrison's poem with its snappy rhyming couplets seems positively jaunty; he employs internal rhyme – 'charred Iraqi' – and alliteration – 'closely clasped creating' – and a very regular rhythm to produce something like doggerel as though the subject is too obscene and grotesque to be permitted the beauty of real art.

Slangy expressions and crude sexual terms are also a device Harrison uses. He makes puns with the line from T. S. Eliot 'A cold coming we had of it' and talks about the American soldiers' 'frozen wad'. In doing this he deliberately provokes the reader into initially condemning such bad taste in 'poetry' but hopefully then being jarred into realizing that squeamishness at vulgarity is an inappropriate response in the face of the material.

Another way Harrison shocks us is with the equation 'one tube' of semen equals all the Iraqui nation – such mind-boggling scientific statistics remind us of the inequality of forces – Iraqi flesh and blood pitted against millions of dollars' worth of scientific excellence.

Up to this point in the poem Harrison has led us to see him as a reasonably genuine narrator – so perhaps we are sufficiently convinced to follow him as he wanders off into classical literature, ignoring the dead soldier's angry words. Sophocles's consolation 'the best of fates is not to be' is then shattered with the words addressed to the narrator and us, 'I never thought life futile, fool.' Only now does Harrison employ more conventional poetic language – the Iraqui soldier was 'filled with such a yearning' and his greatest wish was 'to have engendered there / a child untouched by war's despair' – a poignant moment of genuine emotion.

Finally Harrison's language very directly refers to some of the cliches of war that had become current at the time and allowed people not to confront the reality of what they or their governments were doing. 'Kicking ass' is a lighthearted expression for attempting world domination by means of killing soldiers and civilians.

Swift's use of satire is strikingly different – he does shock but more subtly. Using Gulliver's words he starts off in a beguilingly calm matter-of-fact way – but the reader is instantly amazed that Gulliver can utter such appalling truths without appreciating the awfulness of what he is saying.

> *Differences in opinions hath cost many millions of lives: for instance, whether <u>flesh</u> be <u>bread</u>, or <u>bread</u> be <u>flesh</u>; whether the juice of a certain <u>berry</u> be <u>blood</u> or <u>wine</u>; whether <u>whistling</u> be a vice or a virtue; whether it be better to <u>kiss a post</u>, or throw it into the fire . . . with many more.*

Gulliver naively presents religious differences in literal terms: 'whether the juice of a certain berry be blood or wine'. Swift the clergyman makes two points here, the obvious contradiction inherent in killing people in the name of religion and also the observation that much religion is simply empty superstition and ritual.

From his calm opening Gulliver appears to get carried away with his explanation. As the pace quickens the bland surface is lost and Swift introduces more forceful language, he speaks of people 'wasted by famine' and 'destroyed by pestilence'. The sentences become longer and more convoluted, the terms more exalted. 'It is a very kingly, honourable and frequent practice . . .'

Gulliver is interrupted as he is describing the causes of war by the Houyhnhnm whom we imagine will express the reader's horror and disgust. But to our surprise instead we are told that humans are not physically capable of real savagery – Swift achieves a point that is both amusing and bitterly ironic. This propels Gulliver into a boasting of man's advancements in killing, a list of horrifying achievements:

> *And, being no stranger to the art of war, I gave him a description of cannons, culverins, muskets, carabines, pistols, bullets, powder, swords, bayonets, battles, . . . and . . . I assured him that I had seen them blow up a hundred enemies at once in a siege, and as many in a ship, and beheld the dead bodies drop down in pieces from the clouds . . .*

Swift ends Gulliver's ranting with the comments of the Houyhnhnm and a savage, if reasoned, condemnation not in the end of war itself but the creature which brought war about.

This brings me to my conclusion. Both texts are satirical examinations of war, both aim to shock, go beyond decency, good taste and mere entertainment but I consider most readers of Harrison's poem can easily work out their place between the soldier/victim and the slightly unconcerned narrator – they feel anger, horror and disgust – 'Nation x shouldn't have got involved, the war shouldn't have continued to that extent, or been fought for that reason' but they probably feel more self-righteous than ashamed. Whereas it is impossible to read this section from 'Gulliver's Travels' without feeling implicated. We cannot escape the fact that we understand Gulliver, we <u>are</u> Gulliver and by extension Yahoos, however much we respond to the horse's words. And Swift is great enough, ambiguous enough, to be us, Gulliver, Yahoo and Houyhnhnm.

Patricia

Examiner's comments

- It is clear that Patricia was engaged by these texts. Her answer is thoughtful and conveys a strong personal response.
- She is successful in linking and contrasting the two texts. Her conclusion makes a particularly interesting point of comparison, when she suggests the ways she would expect readers to respond to each of the texts.
- She provides examples of how each writer uses language. The quotations are well-chosen and she analyses details, though she does this more fully when she deals with the Harrison than with the Swift, where some of her points remain a little general. One or two quotations could be more neatly incorporated into her writing.
- While she clearly uses the quotation and question as her starting point, she could have kept these in mind rather more consistently. There are a few places where she could have pointed out more clearly how they relate to her chosen texts and although her conclusion is effective, a final reference to the quotation might give the essay more shape.
- She could also, perhaps, have explored a little more fully the ways that these texts exemplify satire as a genre.
- Her written style is strong and secure and her vocabulary varied, making this a clear and interesting essay to read.

3

Language Barriers

Throughout human history, conflict has been caused or exacerbated by people simply not understanding each other. Individuals, or entire nations, struggle to communicate when they don't 'speak the same language', either literally or metaphorically. The biblical book of Genesis offers a story to explain the separation of humanity into races and the diversity of human language: our inability to understand one another, we are told, results from the sons of men getting above themselves. Once, when they were united in language and purpose, they tried to 'reach unto heaven', to trespass on God's territory, and so He took them down a peg.

The Tower of Babel

And the whole earth was of one language, and of one speech. And it came to pass, as [Noah's descendants] journeyed from the east, that they found a plain in the land of Shinar; and they dwelt there. And they said one to another, Go to, let us make brick, and burn them thoroughly. And they had brick for stone, and slime had they for morter. And they said, Go to, let us build a city and a tower, whose top may reach unto heaven; and let us make us a name, lest we be scattered abroad upon the face of the whole earth. And the LORD came down to see the city and the tower, which the children of men builded. And the LORD said, Behold, the people is one, and they have all one language; and this they begin to do: and now nothing will be restrained from them, which they have imagined to do. Go to, let us go down, and there confound their language, that they may not understand one another's speech. So the LORD scattered them abroad from thence upon the face of all the earth: and they left off to build the city. Therefore is the name of it called Babel; because the LORD did there confound the language of all the earth: and from thence did the LORD scatter them abroad upon the face of all the earth.

Genesis 11
The Bible: Old Testament, Authorized Version

Whatever the explanation, differences in language make it difficult for human beings to fully understand each other. Different languages grow out of different cultures – language itself is a way of making sense of our experience as human beings. If our experiences differ widely, misunderstandings may lie at a level deeper than that of words. Barriers can arise not only between races, but also between people of different social class, gender, or age.

While language may both connect and divide people, it can also represent those connections and divisions symbolically. Since language is the medium writers work with, it is not surprising that they often explore ways in which it reflects and affects human relationships.

Post-colonialism

Language is a particular issue when a dominant nation has colonized another, appropriating territory for itself and imposing its culture on the native population. Following the earliest voyages of 'discovery' of the fifteenth century, Europeans colonized the Americas, Africa, India, Australia and the West Indies. Imperialism reached its height in the nineteenth century but broke down in the twentieth, as more and more nations claimed their independence.

Situations where colonial powers have been driven out and people are seeking to reassert their own cultural identity are sometimes referred to as 'post-colonial'. These cultures are inevitably complex mixtures, often scarred by oppression. A 'pure' form of the original culture cannot be recreated, as the influence of the power that has dominated it cannot be entirely erased.

Studying English Literature at A Level, you are likely to encounter some 'post-colonial' texts in which language is a theme or an issue. These may be by writers whose first language was not English, but who had to learn it in order to survive or make any progress under colonial rule. Other writers may never have spoken the language of their forebears but be conscious of being separated from their 'roots'.

There are a few points to keep in mind when you are studying texts from this sort of context:

- In order to develop your awareness of **context**, it is worth finding out what you can about the cultural background to texts you read. If you are working with an unseen text, take notice of any information you are given about its context and look out for clues in the text itself.
- Look also for clues about the writer's **position**, **viewpoint**, or **attitude**, in relation to his or her culture.
- Literature that is post-colonial, or focuses on language differences, usually addresses issues to do with **identity** and the use of **power**. Messages may be strongly **political**. Become as aware as you can of your own background, beliefs and attitudes and of how these can affect your judgements of what you read.
- Try to get to know something about the many **varieties** and **non-standard** forms of English. Think also about the differences between **spoken** and **written** language. You may encounter the following.
  - Writers' attempts to reproduce regional **accents** or **dialects** in writing. A dialect has special vocabulary or grammatical features, while an accent is a local variation in how a language is pronounced. Look at

how Emily Brontë tries to replicate Yorkshire dialect for the character Joseph in *Wuthering Heights*, for example.

- **Creole** or **pidgin** languages. A *pidgin* is a simplified combination of two languages, which usually developed originally to enable people of different races to communicate and trade with each other. When a language like this has developed and become established, it is known as a *creole*.

- Other variant forms of English which are languages in their own right, with their own grammatical rules and vocabulary, such as **Black English**.

- Literature in **translation** from another language, or where writers are not writing in their first language. Sometimes it is difficult to translate concepts from one language to another; if cultures are very different, translators may struggle to find equivalent vocabulary to express some ideas. You might detect signs of this in some texts.

- Work by writers who portray **oral cultures**, where language takes only a spoken, not a written form. Two authors, Chinua Achebe and Ngugi wa Thiong'o write about this situation in the extracts that follow.

The Tempest

Shakespeare's *The Tempest* has sometimes been said by modern critics to be an example of 'colonialism'. In the play Prospero, formerly Duke of Milan, has escaped from his enemies with his daughter Miranda to a small island, where he now holds power over the only other inhabitant, Caliban. Caliban is apparently only part human. While Shakespeare had read about 'voyages of discovery', colonies and 'cannibals', and used this knowledge in creating the play, there is no evidence that he intended Caliban (Cannibal?) to be seen as a wronged, innocent native who has had his territory usurped by the invader, Prospero. Some modern critics, however, have found him useful as a symbolic figure to illustrate their points of view.

In the extract that follows, Prospero and Miranda talk with Caliban, who is now their slave.

Act 1 Scene 2

Prospero: Come on;
We'll visit Caliban, my slave, who never
Yields us kind answer.
Miranda: 'Tis a villain, sir,
I do not love to look on.
Prospero: But, as 'tis,

We cannot miss him. He does make our fire,
Fetch in our wood, and serves in offices
That profit us. What, ho! Slave! Caliban!
Thou earth, thou, speak!

Caliban: *(within)*   There's wood enough within.

Prospero: Come forth, I say! There's other business for thee.
Come, thou tortoise! When?
*(Enter **Ariel** like a water-nymph)*
Fine apparition! My quaint Ariel,
Hark in thine ear.

Ariel: My lord, it shall be done. *(Exit)*

Prospero: Thou poisonous slave, got by the devil himself
Upon thy wicked dam, come forth!
*(Enter **Caliban**)*

Caliban: As wicked dew as e'er my mother brushed
With raven's feather from unwholesome fen
Drop on you both. A south-west blow on ye
And blister you all o'er.

Prospero: For this, be sure, tonight thou shalt have cramps,
Side-stitches that shall pen thy breath up. Urchins
Shall forth at vast of night that they may work
All exercise on thee. Thou shalt be pinched
As thick as honey-comb, each pinch more stinging
Than bees that made 'em.

Caliban: I must eat my dinner.
This island's mine, by Sycorax my mother,
Which thou tak'st from me. When thou cam'st first,
Thou strok'st me, and made much of me, wouldst give me
Water with berries in't, and teach me how
To name the bigger light, and how the less,
That burn by day and night. And then I loved thee,
And showed thee all the qualities o'th'isle,
The fresh springs, brine-pits, barren place and fertile.
Cursed be I that did so! All the charms
Of Sycorax – toads, beetles, bats, light on you!
For I am all the subjects that you have,
Which first was mine own king; and here you sty me
In this hard rock, whiles you do keep from me
The rest o'th'island.

Prospero: Thou most lying slave,
Whom stripes may move, not kindness! I have used thee,
Filth as thou art, with human care, and lodged thee
In mine own cell, till thou didst seek to violate
The honour of my child.

Caliban: O ho, O ho! Would't had been done!
Thou didst prevent me. I had peopled else
This isle with Calibans.

Miranda:	Abhorred slave
	Which any print of goodness wilt not take,
	Being capable of all ill! I pitied thee,
	Took pains to make thee speak, taught thee each hour
	One thing or other. When thou didst not, savage,
	Know thine own meaning, but wouldst gabble like
	A thing most brutish, I endowed thy purposes
	With words that made them known. But thy vile race,
	Though thou didst learn, had that in't which good natures
	Could not abide to be with. Therefore wast thou
	Deservedly confined into this rock, who hadst
	Deserved more than a prison.
Caliban:	You taught me language, and my profit on't
	Is, I know how to curse. The red plague rid you
	For learning me your language!
Prospero:	Hag-seed, hence!
	Fetch us in fuel – and be quick, thou'rt best,
	To answer other business. Shrug'st thou, malice?
	If thou neglect'st, or dost unwillingly
	What I command, I'll rack thee with old cramps,
	Fill all thy bones with aches, make thee roar,
	That beasts shall tremble at thy din.
Caliban:	No, pray thee!
	(*aside*) I must obey. His art is of such power,
	It would control my dam's god Setebos,
	And make a vassal of him.
Prospero:	So, slave. Hence! (*Exit* **Caliban**)

William Shakespeare

ACTIVITY

1. How does Shakespeare present the relationships between Prospero, Miranda and Caliban here? Look at the language and actions of all three characters.
2. We learn that Miranda taught Caliban 'how to speak'. Make a note of other references to language in the extract. Discuss the ways in which language itself is significant in this situation.
3. In writing, explore the ways in which Shakespeare presents ideas about power and language through his characterization in this extract.

Things Fall Apart

In his first novel, *Things Fall Apart*, the Nigerian writer Chinua Achebe (born in 1930) reveals how the community and traditions of an Ibo tribal village break down when outsiders arrive and impose alien ideas. In doing so, he takes on the challenge of presenting a culture that has a purely oral tradition through the medium of writing.

Here, missionaries begin to introduce the villagers to the Christian faith. As they do not speak the local language, they must communicate through an interpreter.

The arrival of the missionaries had caused a considerable stir in the village of Mbanta. There were six of them and one was a white man. Every man and woman came out to see the white man. Stories about these strange men had grown since one of them had been killed in Abame and his iron horse tied to the sacred silk-cotton tree. And so everybody came to see the white man. It was the time of year when everybody was at home. The harvest was over.

When they had all gathered, the white man began to speak to them. He spoke through an interpreter who was an Ibo man, though his dialect was different and harsh to the ears of Mbanta. Many people laughed at his dialect and the way he used words strangely. Instead of saying 'myself' he always said 'my buttocks'. But he was a man of commanding presence and the clansmen listened to him. He said he was one of them, as they could see from his colour and his language. The other four black men were also their brothers, although one of them did not speak Ibo. The white man was also their brother because they were all sons of God. And he told them about this new God, the Creator of all the world and all the men and women. He told them that they worshipped false gods, gods of wood and stone. A deep murmur went through the crowd when he said this. He told them that the true God lived on high and that all men when they died went before Him for judgment. Evil men and all the heathen who in their blindness bowed to wood and stone were thrown into a fire that burned like palm-oil. But good men who worshipped the true God lived forever in His happy kingdom. 'We have been sent by this great God to ask you to leave your wicked ways and false gods and turn to Him so that you may be saved when you die,' he said.

'Your buttocks understand our language,' said someone lightheartedly and the crowd laughed.

'What did he say?' the white man asked his interpreter. But before he could answer, another man asked a question: 'Where is the white man's horse?' he asked. The Ibo evangelists consulted among themselves and decided that the man probably meant bicycle. They told the white man and he smiled benevolently.

'Tell them,' he said, 'that I shall bring many iron horses when we have settled down among them. Some of them will even ride the iron horse themselves.' This was interpreted to them but very few of them heard. They were talking excitedly among themselves because the white man had said he was going to live among them. They had not thought about that.

At this point, an old man said he had a question. 'Which is this god of yours,' he asked, 'the goddess of the earth, the god of the sky, Amadiora of the thunderbolt, or what?'

The interpreter spoke to the white man and he immediately gave his answer. 'All the gods you have named are not gods at all. They are gods of deceit who tell you to kill your fellows and destroy innocent children. There is only one true God and He has the earth, the sky, you and me and all of us.'

'If we leave our gods and follow your god,' asked another man, 'who will protect us from the anger of our neglected gods and ancestors?'

'Your gods are not alive and cannot do you any harm,' replied the white man. 'They are pieces of wood and stone.'

When this was interpreted to the men of Mbanta they broke into derisive laughter. These men must be mad, they said to themselves. How else could they say that Ani and Amadiora were harmless? And Idemili and Ogwuwu too? And some of them began to go away.

Then the missionaries burst into song. It was one of those gay and rollicking tunes of evangelism which had the power of plucking at silent and dusty chords in the heart of an Ibo man. The interpreter explained each verse to the audience, some of whom now stood enthralled. It was a story of brothers who lived in darkness and in fear, ignorant of the love of God. It told of one sheep out on the hills, away from the gates of God and from the tender shepherd's care.

After the singing the interpreter spoke about the Son of God whose name was Jesu Kristi. Okonkwo, who only stayed in the hope that it might come to chasing the men out of the village or whipping them, now said:

'You told us with your own mouth that there was only one god. Now you talk about his son. He must have a wife, then.' The crowd agreed.

'I did not say He had a wife,' said the interpreter, somewhat lamely.

'Your buttocks said he had a son,' said the joker. 'So he must have a wife and all of them must have buttocks.'

The missionary ignored him and went on to talk about the Holy Trinity. At the end of it Okonkwo was fully convinced that the man was mad. He shrugged his shoulders and went away to tap his afternoon palm-wine.

Chinua Achebe

ACTIVITY

1 How does Achebe present
    a) the missionaries?
    b) the villagers?
    c) their attitudes and responses to one another, and how are these revealed in their speech?

2 Discuss the style of Achebe's writing. What, if anything, suggests that he is using the *written* word to tell his story rather as it might be told in an *oral* culture? You may, for example, notice a quality of directness or simplicity in the writing. This may not be as straightforward as it seems. What is the effect of presenting a situation like this in an *apparently* naive or innocent way? Does it influence your response to the characters in any way?

Student response

Here is Emma's response to the first two preparatory questions on the extract from *Things Fall Apart*. When you have discussed the extract and made your own notes or written responses, compare them with what follows. What do you think are the strengths of her work? What could be improved?

---

a) Chinua Achebe writes in an <u>unbiased fashion and presents the missionaries as the Ibo society would have accepted them</u>.

Although the missionaries were attempting to impose alien ideas among the villagers of Mbanta, a large crowd was attracted. Achebe explains that 'a considerable stir' was caused because of the presence of 'the white man'. Many of the villagers would not have seen a man of another colour or language.

Even though Achebe's <u>methods of writing seem fair</u>, he does manage to make fun of the missionaries in the way he presents the interpreter. 'His dialect was . . . harsh to the ear of Mbanta', and 'instead of saying "myself" he always said "my buttocks"'. This makes to ridicule him and is used as a joke against him by one villager.

The white missionary <u>bombards his audience with definate statements</u>, telling them what they worshipped was wrong. Achebe involves the Ibo translation of a bicycle, 'an iron horse', to emphasize the difference in cultures. When 'the white man' discovers this confusion Achebe makes him appear smug and superior to the Ibos as he 'smiled benevolently'.

The missionaries begin to realize that their tactics aren't working and many of the crowd are dispersing and decide to 'burst into song'. Achebe writes that the song was 'gay and rollicking' and it made some of its audience stand 'enthralled'.

Achebe doesn't give any direct criticisms or appraisals about the missionaries, but guides the reader into thinking that they are cunning and professional about converting others to Christianity.

b) Achebe presents the villagers of Mbanta to be inquisitive about the missionaries. 'Stories about these strange men', meaning white men, had enticed everybody from their compound. The villagers are also portrayed to be naive and some of them easily led. Achebe manipulates the story of the 'iron horse' or bicycle to emphasize the cultural difference and the ni<u>a</u>vety of the Ibo society.

Some of Mbanta actually listen to the preachings of the missionaries. Achebe makes them appear fickle in their decisions by doing this, because beliefs of their own Gods were in-bred, and suddenly some one changes their minds as to the way they have thought their whole life.

Achebe shows that the Ibos aren't taking too serious_, though, when one jokes that the interpreter's 'buttocks understand our language', to emphasize the difficulty in translation. Also when they are told that their existing Gods could cause them no harm because they are not alive, the villagers 'broke into derisive laughter'.

> Okonkwo represents his village when he challenges the interpreter about God's son, saying he must have a wife and therefore there must be a Goddess, contradicting the whole point that there is only one God.
>
> Okonkwo concludes that the missionaries must be insane and dismisses them completely.
>
> *Emma*

Examiner's comments

- Emma's answers so far are quite perceptive. The points she makes about both missionaries and villagers show – implicitly if not always explicitly – that she is thinking about the situation and aware of the kind of context in which this incident might have taken place. She makes this clear in her opening paragraphs.

- She begins to explore Achebe's style and to show some understanding of the tone of the writing and the attitude it conveys, for example when she points out how Achebe makes the missionary appear 'smug and superior'.

- Some of her best points need further development, however; I have underlined some places where she could improve her answer by exploring or explaining her ideas in more depth and detail. For example, her opening statement that Achebe 'writes in an unbiased fashion' is interesting and valid. She refers to the idea again when she tells us that his 'methods of writing seem fair', but she doesn't follow this up with a more precise explanation of what she means, or provide any evidence from the text to support her assertion. Later in her answer she returns to the point once more and just begins to explore it when she says 'Achebe doesn't give any direct criticisms or appraisals about the missionaries', but still doesn't develop the idea as much as she could.

- She does demonstrate that she can read closely, paying attention to details. Her examples from the text are well-chosen and she has mastered the skill of embedding short quotations in her writing. She could now go on to make more use of her quotations, analysing them more closely and ensuring that she shows how and why particular words and phrases create certain effects. For example, her good point that the missionary appeared 'smug and superior to the Ibos as he "smiled benevolently"' could be taken further with some probing of the word 'benevolently' and the reason why it has negative connotations here.

- There are also a few places where further quotations would be useful, particularly in her last few paragraphs where she points out the different reactions of Okonkwo and Nwoye, but does not refer to the text.

- On a technical note, her style is clear and usually conveys her meaning. One paragraph, where she tries to explain how the Ibo 'appear fickle in their decisions' could be expressed better, and she does need to avoid making small, careless errors with spelling.

• Overall, this is promising work, showing skills and understanding on which she can build.

Translations

Brian Friel's play *Translations*, first performed in 1980, is set in Baile Beag, an Irish-speaking village in County Donegal, in the 1830s. Cartographers from the English army have been given the task of surveying and mapping Ireland. In the process, Irish (Gaelic) place names are to be 'translated' into English. A map of Ireland with English place names is an obvious symbol of colonialism – a dominant power obliterating a native language and culture. The play is written in English, but we have to imagine that the characters who speak only Gaelic are speaking their own language. They do not understand the English-speaking characters, and vice versa.

In this scene, Owen, a young man from Baile Beag who does speak both English and Gaelic, introduces two of the English officers to the local people who study at the Hedge School run by his father, Hugh, and older brother, Manus. Some of them have learned Latin, but not English.

Act I

(**Owen** *is the younger son, a handsome, attractive young man in his twenties. He is dressed smartly – a city man. His manner is easy and charming: everything he does is invested with consideration and enthusiasm. . . . [He] enters with* **Lancey** *and* **Yolland**. **Captain Lancey** *is middle-aged; a small, crisp officer, expert in his field as cartographer but uneasy with people – especially civilians, especially these foreign civilians. His skill is with deeds, not words.* **Lieutenant Yolland** *is in his late twenties/early thirties. He is tall and thin and gangling, blond hair, a shy, awkward manner. A soldier by accident.*)

Owen:	Here we are. Captain Lancey – my father.
Lancey:	Good evening.
	(**Hugh** *becomes expansive, almost courtly, with his visitors.*)
Hugh:	You and I have already met, sir.
Lancey:	Yes.
Owen:	And Lieutenant Yolland both Royal engineers – my father.
Hugh:	You're very welcome, gentlemen.
Yolland:	How do you do.
Hugh:	*Gaudeo vos hic adesse. [Welcome.]*
Owen:	And I'll make no other introductions except that these are some of the people of Baile Beag and – what? – well you're among the best people in Ireland now. (*He pauses to allow* **Lancey** *to speak.* **Lancey** *does not.*) Would you like to say a few words, Captain?

Hugh:	What about a drop, sir?
Lancey:	A what?
Hugh:	Perhaps a modest refreshment? A little sampling of our aqua vitae?
Lancey:	No, no.
Hugh:	Later, perhaps when . . .
Lancey:	I'll say what I have to say, if I may, and as briefly as possible. Do they speak *any* English, Roland?
Owen:	Don't worry, I'll translate.
Lancey:	I see. (*He clears his throat. He speaks as if he were addressing children – a shade too loudly and enunciating excessively.*) You may have seen me – seen me – working in this section – section? – working. We are here – here – in this place – you understand? – to make a map – a map – a map and –
Jimmy:	*Nonne Latine loquitur?* [*Does he not speak Latin?*] (**Hugh** *holds up a restraining hand.*)
Hugh:	James.
Lancey:	(*To* **Jimmy**) I do not speak Gaelic, sir. (*He looks at* **Owen**.)
Owen:	Carry on.
Lancey:	A map is a representation on paper – a picture – you understand picture? – a paper picture – showing, representing this country – yes? – showing your country in miniature – a scaled drawing on paper of – of – of – (*Suddenly* **Doalty** *sniggers. Then* **Bridget**. *Then* **Sarah**. **Owen** *leaps in quickly.*)
Owen:	It might be better if you *assume* they understand you –
Lancey:	Yes?
Owen:	And I'll translate as you go along.
Lancey:	I see. Yes. Very well. Perhaps you're right. Well. What we are doing is this. (*He looks at* **Owen**. **Owen** *nods reassuringly.*) His Majesty's government has ordered the first ever comprehensive survey of this entire country – a general triangulation which will embrace detailed hydrographic and topographic information and which will be executed to a scale of six inches to the English mile.
Hugh:	(*Pouring a drink.*) Excellent – excellent. (**Lancey** *looks at* **Owen**.)
Owen:	A new map is being made of the whole country. (**Lancey** *looks to* **Owen**: *Is that all?* **Owen** *smiles reassuringly and indicates to proceed.*)
Lancey:	This enormous task has been embarked on so that the military authorities will be equipped with up-to-date and accurate information on every corner of this part of the Empire.
Owen:	The job is being done by soldiers because they are skilled in this work.
Lancey:	And also so that the entire basis of land valuation can be reassessed for purposes of more equitable taxation.

Owen:	This new map will take the place of the estate-agent's map so that from now on you will know exactly what is yours in law.
Lancey:	In conclusion I wish to quote two brief extracts from the white paper which is our governing charter: (*Reads*) 'All former surveys of Ireland originated in forfeiture and violent transfer of property; the present survey has for its object the relief which can be afforded to the proprietors and occupiers of land from unequal taxation.'
Owen:	The captain hopes that the public will cooperate with the sappers and that the new map will mean that taxes are reduced.
Hugh:	A worthy enterprise – *opus honestum!* And Extract B.
Lancey:	'Ireland is privileged. No such survey is being undertaken in England. So this survey cannot but be received as proof of the disposition of this government to advance the interests of Ireland.' My sentiments too.
Owen:	This survey demonstrates the government's interest in Ireland and the captain thanks you for listening so attentively to him.
Hugh:	Our pleasure, Captain.
Lancey:	Lieutenant Yolland?
Yolland:	I – I – I've nothing to say – really –
Owen:	The captain is the man who actually makes the new map. George's task is to see that the place-names on this map are correct. (*To* **Yolland**.) Just a few words – they'd like to hear you. (*To class.*) Don't you want to hear George, too?
Maire:	Has he anything to say?
Yolland:	(*To* **Maire**) Sorry – sorry?
Owen:	She says she's dying to hear you.
Yolland:	(*To* **Maire**) Very kind of you – thank you . . . (*To class.*) I can only say that I feel – I feel very foolish to – to – to – be working here and not to speak your language. But I intend to rectify that – with Roland's help – indeed I do.
Owen:	He wants me to teach him Irish!
Hugh:	You are doubly welcome, sir.
Yolland:	I think your countryside is – is – is – is very beautiful. I've fallen in love with it already. I hope we're not too – too crude an intrusion on your lives. And I know that I'm going to be happy, very happy here.
Owen:	He is already a committed Hibernophile –
Jimmy:	He loves –
Owen:	Alright, Jimmy – we know – he loves Baile Beag; and he loves you all.

Brian Friel

ACTIVITY
1 Working in a group, experiment with reading/acting the extract.
2 Discuss how, in performance, the language difference might be conveyed effectively, bearing in mind that both English- and Gaelic-speaking parts are

written in English. Make notes, or annotate the text with additional stage directions.

3 Discuss how you would expect an audience to respond to the various characters in this episode.

4 Write as fully as you can about the similarities and differences between extracts B and C, comparing the ways Achebe and Friel explore issues such as colonialism and language difference. You could consider:

- how each writer presents different individuals and groups and the relationships between them
- the role of the interpreter in each situation
- how each writer exploits communication difficulties to convey both serious points and a sense of the ridiculous.

Decolonizing the Mind

The next extract is from a non-fiction text by the Kenyan writer Ngugi wa Thiong'o, in which he explores 'the politics of language in African literature'. After writing several successful novels and other books in English, he now writes once more in his own language, Gikuyu. Here he writes autobiographically about the effect on him of an English colonial education.

I was born into a large peasant family: father, four wives and about twenty-eight children. I also belonged, as we all did in those days, to a wider extended family and to the community as a whole.

We spoke Gikuyu as we worked in the fields. We spoke Gikuyu in and outside the home. I can vividly recall those evenings of story-telling around the fireside. It was mostly the grown-ups telling the children but everybody was interested and involved. We children would re-tell the stories the following day to other children who worked in the fields picking the pyrethrum flowers, tea-leaves or coffee beans of our European and African landlords.

The stories, with mostly animals as the main characters, were all told in Gikuyu. Hare, being small, weak but full of innovative wit and cunning, was our hero. We identified with him as he struggled against the brutes of prey like lion, leopard, hyena. His victories were our victories and we learnt that the apparently weak can outwit the strong. We followed the animals in their struggle against hostile nature – drought, rain, sun, wind – a confrontation often forcing them to search for forms of co-operation. But we were also interested in their struggles amongst themselves, and particularly between the beasts and the victims of prey. These twin struggles against nature and other animals, reflected real-life struggles in the human world.

Not that we neglected stories with human beings as the main characters. There were two types of characters in such human-centred narratives: the species of truly human beings with qualities of courage, kindness, mercy, hatred of evil, concern for others; and a man-eat-man two-mouthed species with qualities of greed, selfishness, individualism and hatred of what was good for the larger co-operative community. Co-operation as the ultimate good in a community was a constant theme. It could unite human beings with animals against ogres and beasts of prey, as in the story of how dove, after being fed with castor-oil seeds, was sent to fetch a smith working far away from home and whose pregnant wife was being threatened by these man-eating two-mouthed ogres.

There were good and bad story-tellers. A good one could tell the same story over and over again, and it would always be fresh to us, the listeners. He or she could tell a story told by someone else and make it more alive and dramatic. The differences really were in the use of words and images and the inflexion of voices to effect different tones.

We therefore learnt to value words for their meaning and nuances. Language was not a mere string of words. It had a suggestive power well beyond the immediate and lexical meaning. Our appreciation of the suggestive magical power of language was reinforced by the games we played with words through riddles, proverbs, transpositions of syllables, or through nonsensical but musically arranged words. So we learnt the music of our language on top of the content. The language, through images and symbols, gave us a view of the world, but it had a beauty of its own. The home and the field were then our pre-primary school but what is important, for this discussion, is that the language of our evening teach-ins, and the language of our immediate and wider community, and the language of our work in the fields were one.

And then I went to school, a colonial school, and this harmony was broken. The language of my education was no longer the language of my culture. I first went to Kamaandura, missionary run, and then to another called Maanguuu run by nationalists grouped around the Gikuyu Independent and Karinga Schools Association. Our language of education was still Gikuyu. The very first time I was ever given an ovation for my writing was over a composition in Gikuyu. So for my first four years there was still harmony between the language of my formal education and that of the Limuru peasant community.

It was after the declaration of a state of emergency over Kenya in 1952 that all the schools run by patriotic nationalists were taken over by the colonial regime and were placed under District Education Boards chaired by Englishmen. English became the language of my formal education. In Kenya, English became more than a language: it was *the* language, and all the others had to bow before it in deference.

Thus one of the most humiliating experiences was to be caught speaking Gikuyu in the vicinity of the school. The culprit was given corporal punishment – three to five strokes of the cane on bare buttocks – or was made to carry a metal plate around the neck with inscriptions such as I AM STUPID or I AM A DONKEY. Sometimes the culprits were fined money they could hardly afford. And how did the teachers catch the culprits? A button was initially given to one pupil, who was supposed to hand it over to whoever was caught speaking his mother tongue. Whoever had the button at the end of the day would sing who had given it to him and the ensuing process would bring out all the culprits of the day. Thus children were turned into witch-hunters and in the process were being taught the lucrative value of being a traitor to one's immediate community.

The attitude to English was the exact opposite: any achievement in spoken or written English was highly rewarded; prizes, prestige, applause; the ticket to higher realms. English became the measure of intelligence and ability in the arts, the sciences, and all the other branches of learning. English became the main determinant of a child's progress up the ladder of formal education.

Ngugi wa Thiong'o

ACTIVITY

1 Discuss the points Ngugi wa Thiong'o makes about the differences between his education in his native language and his education in English. Think about
   • the values and messages of the stories of his childhood;
   • the messages children received about themselves and their language once they began their English education.
2 Write an assessment of the passage, exploring what it has to tell us about language and culture and relating it to one or more of the other texts in this unit.

E

Hindi Urdu Bol Chaal

Moniza Alvi was born in Lahore, Pakistan, in 1954, but moved to England when she was only a few months old and did not revisit Pakistan until 1993. She says, 'I think it's important to know what has gone into your making, even quite far back, I think it gives you a sense perhaps of richness. And I found it was important to write the Pakistan poems because I was getting in touch with my background.' This poem is from the collection *A Bowl of Warm Air*, published in 1996.

The author Moniza Alvi

(*bol chaal:* dialogue)

These are languages I try to touch
as if my tongue is a fingertip gently
matching its whorls to echoings of sound.

Separating Urdu from Hindi – it's like
sifting grains of wild rice
or separating India from Pakistan.

The sign of nasal intonation
floats like a heat haze
above new words.

Words like hands banging on the table.

*

I introduce myself to two languages,
but there are so many – of costume,
of conduct and courtesy.

I listen hard as if to sense minute changes of dialect from village to village
from West Punjab to West Bengal.

These languages could have been mine –
the whisper of silks on silks
and the slapping and patting of chapattis on the tava.

*

I imagine the meetings and greetings
in Urdu borrowed from Sanskrit,
Arabic and Persian.

I shall be borrowed from England.
Pakistan, assalaam alaikum –
Peace be with you – Helloji.

It is not you I am meeting.
It is a sound system travelling through
countries, ascending and descending

in ragas, drumbeats, clapping.

*

In Lahore there grows a language tree
its roots branching to an earlier time
its fruit ripe, ready to fall.

I hear the rustling of mango groves
my living and dead relatives
quarrelling together and I search

for a nugget of sound, the kernel
of language. I am enlarged
by what I cannot hear –

the village conferences, the crackling
of bonfires and the rap of gunfire.

*

My senses stir with words
that must be reinvented.
At the market I'll ask *How much?*

and wait for just one new word
to settle like a stone
at the bottom of a well.

Moniza Alvi

ACTIVITY
1   Make notes on the images Alvi uses to describe the experience of hearing
     and trying to understand different languages.
2   Write a detailed critical appreciation of the poem.

Lastly, two Caribbean poets use a more humorous approach to make serious
points about 'language barriers'. Valerie Bloom, a Jamaican poet born in
1956 uses a creole language, while John Agard, who was born in Guyana in
1949 but now lives in England, writes in English inflected with Caribbean
creole. In both cases, the sound of the words is important for a full
understanding, so either read them aloud or at least try to imagine the sound
of them.

Language Barrier

Jamaica language sweet yuh know bwoy,
An yuh know mi nebba notice i',
Till tarra day one foreign frien
Come spen some time wid mi.

An den im call mi attention to
Some tings im sey soun' queer,
Like de way wi always sey 'koo yah'
When we really mean 'look here'.

Den anodda ting whey puzzle im,
Is how wi lub 'repeat' wise'f
For de ongle time im repeat a wud
Is when smaddy half deaf.

Todda day im walk outa road
An when im a pass one gate,

Im see one bwoy a one winda,
An one nodda one outside a wait.

Im sey dem did look kine o'nice
Soh im ben a go sey howdy,
But im tap shart when de fus' bwoy sey
'A ready yuh ready aready?'

Den like sey dat ney quite enuff,
Fe po' likkle foreign Hugh,
Him hear de nedda bwoy halla out,
'A come mi come fe come wait fe yuh'.

An dat is nat all dat puzzle him,
Why wi run wi words togedda?
For when im expec' fe hear 'the other',
Him hear dis one word, 'todda'.

Instead o'wi sey 'all of you'
Wi ongle sey unoo,
Him can dis remember sey
De wud fe 'screech owl' is 'patoo'.

As fe some expression him hear,
Im wouldn badda try meck dem out,
Like 'boonoonoonos,' 'chamba-chamba,'
An ''kibba up yuh mout'.

Him can hardly see de connection,
Between 'only' and 'dengey',
An im woulda like fe meet de smaddy
Who invent de wud 'preckey'.

Mi advise im no fe fret imself,
For de Spaniards do it to,
For when dem mean fe sey 'jackass',
Dem always sey 'burro'.

De French, Italian, Greek an Dutch,
Dem all guilty o' de crime
None a dem no chat im language,
Soh Hugh betta larn fe mime.

But sayin' dis an dat yuh know,
Some o' wi cyan eben undastan one anodda,
Eben doah wi all lib yah
An chat de same patois.

For from las' week mi a puzzzle out,
Whey Joey coulda mean,
When im teck im facey self soh ax
Ef any o' im undapants clean.

Valerie Bloom

Listen Mr Oxford Don

Me not no Oxford don
me a simple immigrant
from Clapham Common
I didn't graduate
I immigrate

But listen Mr Oxford don
I'm a man on de run
and a man on de run
is a dangerous one

I ent have no gun
I ent have no knife
but mugging de Queen's English
is the story of my life

I dont need no axe
to spilt/ up yu syntax
I dont need no hammer
to mash/ up yu grammar

I warning you Mr Oxford don
I'm a wanted man
and a wanted man
is a dangerous one

Dem accuse me of assault
on de Oxford dictionary/
imagine a concise peaceful man like me/
dem want me serve time
for inciting rhyme to riot
but I tekking it quiet
down here in Clapham Common

I'm not a violent man Mr Oxford don
I only armed wit mih human breath
but human breath
is a dangerous weapon

So mek dem send one big word after me
I ent serving no jail sentence
I slashing suffix in self-defence
I bashing future wit present tense
and if necessary

I making de Queen's English accessory/
to my offence

John Agard

ACTIVITY

1 Experiment with reading the poems aloud; if you can, listen to the work of Caribbean poets on tape, or even better, in live performance.
2 Discuss the points that each of these poets makes about language in relation to race, class, power, or politics.
3 How does each use humour to convey these ideas?
4 Make detailed notes on the way each uses language, focusing on vocabulary and imagery as well as the use of non-standard English.
5 Write a detailed critical commentary on one – or both – of the poems.

Language Barriers:

Further activities

1 Choose at least two post-colonial texts from this unit and compare the ways in which they explore the relationship between language and cultural identity. Refer to your own wider reading of post-colonial literature if it is relevant.
2 Language enables us to communicate, but also creates barriers between people. Write in detail about how the writers of three of these texts deal with this issue.
3 Explore the ways writers use humour to make important points in three or more of the texts included here.
4 It is sometimes said that 'Language is power'. To what extent is that reflected in the texts included here? Refer to extract A and at least one other text, either from this selection or from your own reading.

4

The Literature of Love

From the very earliest times writers have shown a deep preoccupation with the idea of 'love' in all its forms. Chaucer's pilgrims exhibit a variety of attitudes towards it, from the courtly idealism of the Knight and the pragmatism of the Wife of Bath, to the earthiness of the Miller. In one form or another love is central to most of Shakespeare's plays; sonnets have been written on it, novels have tried to explore its complexities, plays have parodied attitudes towards it, and still it is of continuing interest to writers and readers alike.

Of course, we should not be surprised by this because love is a basic human emotion that we all share. It is a common thread that binds us together and allows us to understand and share the experiences of others, despite barriers of class or culture, race or religion, society or time. The commonality of our experience allows us to understand something of what Othello feels in his tormented, jealousy-afflicted love for Desdemona, or what Paul Morel or Miriam feel when he wants to break off his relationship with her.

Of course, love and the situations that it gives rise to in literature can take many forms, and the following extracts present just a small glimpse of some of them.

ACTIVITY Before you read the texts in this unit, discuss some of your own ideas about love and the various attitudes that humans can adopt towards it.

There are many ways in which writers might use language to convey their ideas about love.

- Imagery is often important. Writers frequently use metaphors and similes to capture the nature of love or describe its effects on themselves or others.
- The tone and mood created might be bitter or regretful or joyful, depending on the nature of the writer's experience of, or attitude towards love.
- Personification might be used – quite frequently writers have written about 'Love' as if it is a living thing.
- Look out for the rhythm pattern of the piece of writing. This can influence the writing in an important way.
- The writer's style can affect the way in which you respond to what is written.

We will begin this unit by considering several poems, all on the topic of love but very different in other respects.

Stop All the Clocks

Read the following poem carefully, alone or with a partner. Discuss and make notes on these questions:
1 What event is the poet responding to?
2 How does Auden use language and imagery to convey his feelings here?
3 Make a list of the images used. What do you notice about them?
4 How does the use of rhyme and rhythm add to the impact of the poem?
5 How effective do you find this poem as an expression of feeling? Why?

Stop all the clocks, cut off the telephone,
Prevent the dog from barking with a juicy bone,
Silence the pianos and with muffled drum
Bring out the coffin, let the mourners come.

Let aeroplanes circle moaning overhead
Scribbling on the sky the message He Is Dead,
Put the crepe bows round the white necks of the public doves,
Let the traffic policemen wear black cotton gloves.

He was my North, my South, my East and West,
My working week and my Sunday rest,
My noon, my midnight, my talk, my song;
I thought that love would last for ever: I was wrong.

The stars are not wanted now: put out every one;
Pack up the moon and dismantle the sun;
Pour away the ocean and sweep up the wood.
For nothing now can ever come to any good.

W. H. Auden

Here are some of the points that you may have noticed:

- The poem is an expression of grief at the death of a lover. (You may remember it being recited in the film *Four Weddings and a Funeral.*)
- The poet uses a wide range of imagery to emphasize the enormity of the impact that his lover's death has had on his life. If you listed the images, you might have noticed that in the first two stanzas the images are drawn from everyday life – aeroplanes, policemen, doves, the dog with a bone, and so on. The depth of the tragedy is expressed by what the poet says about these everyday sights being converted to signs of mourning.

- In the following two stanzas the images are drawn from much more 'cosmic' sources – all the points of the compass, the stars, the sun, the moon.
- The form of the poem is quite regular, both in terms of its structure and its rhythm pattern. It is also written in a regular pattern of rhyming couplets. This kind of rhyme scheme is often associated with verse that has a light theme, but here the overall effect is quite different. The apparent restraint of the rhyme and rhythm contrasts with the words and images of the poem to give a sense of someone struggling to restrain emotions, trying to avoid complete breakdown at a time of tragedy.

Now we will look at poem B, *The Parting* and poem C *Time Does Not Bring Relief.*

The Parting

Since there's no help, come let us kiss and part;
Nay, I have done, you get no more of me.
And I am glad, yea, glad with all my heart,
That thus so cleanly I myself can free.
Shake hands for ever, cancel all our vows,
And when we meet at any time again,
Be it not seen in either of our brows
That we one jot of former love retain.
Now at the last gasp of Love's latest breath,
When, his pulse failing, Passion speechless lies,
When Faith is kneeling by his bed of death,
And innocence is closing up his eyes.
Now if thou would'st, when all have given him over,
From death to life thou might'st him yet recover.

Michael Drayton

Time Does Not Bring Relief

Time does not bring relief; you all have lied
Who told me time would ease me of my pain!
I miss him in the weeping of the rain;
I want him at the shrinking of the tide;

The old snows melt from every mountain-side;
And last year's leaves are smoke in every lane;
But last year's bitter loving must remain
Heaped on my heart, and my old thoughts abide.
There are a hundred places where I fear
To go – so with his memory they brim.
And entering with relief some quiet place
Where never fell his foot or shone his face
I say, 'There is no memory of him here!'
And so stand stricken, so remembering him.

Edna St Vincent Millay

ACTIVITY

1 Make notes on the ideas that each poet expresses.
2 What differences exist between the viewpoints of the two poets?
3 Compare the ways in which they use language and imagery to express their ideas.
4 What attitude towards love do you think each poet holds?
5 Compare the effectiveness of each poem, supporting your personal view with reasons.

Student response

Here is how one student responded to the questions above about these poems.

1.

In his poem, 'The Parting', Michael Drayton expresses the following ideas:

- *he can completely detach himself from the memory of a former lover*
- *'love' itself is not always forever*
- *love can be reborn.*

In Edna St Vincent Millay's poem, 'Time Does Not Bring Relief', the following ideas are expressed:

- *the love she had for a former lover cannot be forgotten*
- *there is no escape from the memory of a former lover*
- *time, as a 'healer', is ineffective with love.*

2.

Michael Drayton, in the poem, 'The Parting', appears to suggest that he can completely detach himself from a former love. The line: 'that thus so cleanly I myself can free', suggests that he is somewhat proactive in his detachment and is, therefore, in full control of his emotions. However, by expressing her inability to forget her former love, Edna St Vincent Millay, in the poem, 'Time Does Not Bring Relief', demonstrates a lack of control over her emotions: 'But last year's bitter loving must remain / Heaped on my heart.'

Although the idea of 'escaping' a former love is common to both poems, each poet takes a different viewpoint. Drayton, in a somewhat 'cold' tone, expresses the view that escape is possible and that he can take an active part in ensuring his 'release': 'I have done, you get no more of me.' However, Millay's poem highlights how she cannot escape from the memories of a former love and, therefore, escaping appears to be impossible for her. Throughout the poem we see how she is 'trapped' by her memories. Not only does she remember her former love in places that they have been together: 'There are a hundred places . . . so with his memory they brim', but there is no 'relief' for her in places never visited together: 'There is no memory of him here! / And so stand stricken, so remembering him.' These final two lines also highlight how, unlike Drayton who is active in releasing himself, Millay appears to be at the mercy of her painful memories.

We can also see differences in the poets' viewpoints with regard to the longevity of love. The very title of Millay's poem, 'Time Does Not Bring Relief', states how the passing of time is ineffective in helping her to forget her former love. Throughout the poem there are images of time passing: 'The old snows melt . . . last year's leaves are smoke in every lane', suggesting that her suffering will last an eternity. This suggestion is further enhanced by the line: 'I want him at the shrinking of the tide'. However, by personifying love, Drayton appears to suggest an element of vulnerability and inevitability with regard to love. He endows 'Love' with the vulnerable nature of human existence and the inevitability of death: 'Now at the last gasp of Love's latest breath.'

Although these differences are apparent, perhaps the most fundamental difference between the two poets is their feelings regarding their lost loves. Unlike Millay, who appears to be mournful of her circumstances, Drayton claims to be: 'glad, yea, glad with all my heart'.

3.

Both 'The Parting' and 'Time Does Not Bring Relief' are poems written in sonnet form. They both express an individual thought, expand on this through the body of the poem, and then draw a conclusion in the final two lines. Although Millay's conclusion leaves us with a sense of hopelessness: 'And so stand stricken, so remembering him', Drayton's poem ends with a note of optimism in the possibility of love returning: 'From death to life thou might'st him (Love) yet recover'. However, this optimistic feel is placed in the concluding rhyming couplet which gives a sense of finality.

Both poets use language effectively to support the negative imagery evident in their poems. For instance, in 'Time Does Not Bring Relief', phrases such as the 'weeping of the rain' and 'ease me of my pain' reflects the sadness that the poet is experiencing. In this poem, we see things being in apparent demise or decay which supports the poet's feelings of loss: 'the <u>shrinking</u> of the tide', 'old snows <u>melt</u>', 'last year's leaves are <u>smoke</u> in every lane'. Likewise, Drayton's negative approach is emphasized in his use of the present continuous verb forms when describing the dying of 'Love'. This gives both the sense of movement and an inevitability of Love's death: 'failing', 'kneeling', 'closing'.

It is interesting to see how, whilst Millay expresses her loss through concrete, tangible images such as the 'snow', 'places', 'rain' etc., Drayton employs an abstract approach, relying on the personification of 'Love'. This also emphasizes the contrast between Drayton's apparent detachment from love and Millay's enduring torment of physical pain: 'last year's bitter loving must remain'. The use of alliteration in the final line of Millay's poem: 'And so stand stricken,' must be read with a somewhat abrupt harshness, this being reflective of Millay's realization that there is no escape from her painful memories.

4.

As discussed earlier, Drayton seems to have the attitude that love can be controlled in some way. He appears to be certain that time will not affect his resolution to end his relationship with his lover: 'And when we meet at any time again, / Be it not seen in either of our brows / That we one jot of former love retain.' In addition, he expresses himself coldly: 'Shake hands for ever, cancel all our vows,' thus reinforcing his capacity and determination to be unaffected by his loss. Furthermore, if 'Love' were to return to Drayton's life, it would be at someone else's bidding: '_thou_ might'st him yet recover'.

Millay's attitude too suggests that time will not alter the way she is feeling – although her feelings of sadness stand in stark contrast to those of release expressed by Drayton: 'Time does not bring relief; you all have lied'. However, like Drayton, Millay too appears to make a determined effort to forget her love by seeking out places that hold no memory of her former lover, albeit without much success. The feelings of love, for her, are quite out of her control: 'my old thoughts _must_ abide.' A feeling that it will be a long time before Millay is able to love again is realized.

5.

Both poems appear to be effective in that they express individual ideas which are supported by the images and language contained within them, although the real effectiveness of the sentiments that they express depends on the poets' original intention for writing them. However, on saying this, both poems are successful in being effective as they manage to capture identifiable emotions. For instance, Drayton's expressions of detachment, and the cold tone sensed in his poem, is not an unreasonable response to expect from someone who is creating barriers to avoid suffering the pain of loss. Likewise, most of us have felt the apparent futility in attempting to escape from painful memories such as those expressed in Millay's 'Time Does Not Bring Relief'. However, Millay's response to her loss appears to be more realistic in that, unlike the abstract nature of Drayton's imagery, she expresses her loss through tangible, concrete ideas, thus creating a more plausible response.

Sandra

Examiner's comments

1 The student's notes are brief but perceptive. She sums up the key ideas contained within the poems and sums them up succinctly. The use of bullet points here probably helps the student to isolate her individual points and can provide you with a useful technique to use in tasks such as these.

2 In response to this task the student offers a full response with plenty of detail:

- The response begins by focusing on Drayton's poem and contrasts this to Millay's. The comments are again perceptive and in each case backed up with relevant quotation.
- The second paragraph explores the differences between the two poems further, but begins by identifying a feature common to both – the sense of 'escaping' a former love. Once again, here the student makes some perceptive points, again using quotation to support the ideas.
- The third paragraph deals with another relevant difference of viewpoint and again supports views with references to the text.

Overall this is a perceptive response which focuses clearly on the task and makes some perceptive, well-supported points showing good understanding of the poems.

3 This response also shows good focus.

- Although not really asked about form, the student rightly identifies the fact that both poems are written in the sonnet form and goes on to comment on how this contributes to each poem's development.
- These comments are backed up with a clear focus on the language of the poems. A range of relevant examples are used to illustrate differences between the two poems.

4 This task asked about each poet's attitudes. Again, the student addresses the task directly, contrasting the attitudes of the two poets. She shows a good focus on the language used and the effects created.

5 This paragraph sums up the student's views effectively while at the same time reinforcing, through examples, comments made earlier.

Overall the response shows a maturity of expression and understanding that would indicate a good quality of response to these activities.

We will look at some more poems inspired by thoughts of love a little later. For the moment, though, we will look at how two pairs of Shakespearian characters talk to each other of love.

Romeo and Juliet

In Extract D, from *Romeo and Juliet*, we see Romeo at Juliet's balcony, professing his deep love for her. He had met her only a short time before at a party that Juliet's father, Capulet, had hosted. The Capulets and Romeo's family, the Montagues, are involved in a long-standing and serious family feud, and Juliet is worried for Romeo's safety should any of her family find him there. Romeo, though, shrugs off her complaints.

Act II Scene 1

Romeo: Alack there lies more peril in thine eye
Than twenty of their swords; look thou but sweet,
And I am proof against their enmity.

Juliet: I would not for the world they saw thee here.

Romeo: I have night's cloak to hide me from their eyes,
And but thou love me, let them find me here.
My life were better ended by their hate,
Than death prorogued, wanting of thy love.

Juliet: By whose direction found'st thou out this place?

Romeo: By love, that first did prompt me to inquire;
He lent me counsel, and I lent him eyes.
I am no pilot, yet wert thou as far
As that vast shore washed with the farthest sea,
I should adventure for such merchandise.

Juliet: Thou knowest the mask of night is on my face,
Else would a maiden blush bepaint my cheek,
For that which thou hast heard me speak tonight.
Fain would I dwell on form, fain, fain deny
What I have spoke; but farewell compliment.
Dost thou love me? I know thou wilt say 'Ay',
And I will take thy word. Yet if thou swearest,
Thou mayst prove false; at lovers' perjuries
They say Jove laughs. O gentle Romeo,
If thou dost love, pronounce it faithfully.
Or if thou thinkest I am too quickly won,
I'll frown and be perverse, and say thee nay,
So thou wilt woo; but else not for the world.
In truth, fair Montague, I am too fond,
And therefore thou mayst think my 'haviour light.
But trust me gentleman, I'll prove more true
Than those that have more cunning to be strange.
I should have been more strange, I must confess,
But that thou overheard'st, ere I was ware,

My true-love passion. Therefore pardon me,
And not impute this yielding to light love,
Which the dark night hath so discovered.

Romeo: Lady, by yonder blessed moon I vow,
That tips with silver all these fruit-tree tops –

Juliet: O swear not by the moon, th' inconstant moon,
That monthly changes in her circled orb,
Lest that thy love prove likewise variable.

Romeo: What shall I swear by?

Juliet: Do not swear at all;
Or if thou wilt, swear by thy gracious self,
Which is the god of my idolatry,
And I'll believe thee.

Romeo: If my heart's dear love –

Juliet: Well do not swear. Although I joy in thee,
I have no joy of this contract tonight.
It is too rash, too unadvised, too sudden;
Too like the lightning, which doth cease to be
Ere one can say, 'It lightens'. Sweet, good night.
This bud of love by summer's ripening breath
May prove a beauteous flower when next we meet.
Good night, good night. As sweet response and rest
Come to thy heart, as that within my breast.

Romeo: O wilt thou leave me so unsatisfied?

Juliet: What satisfaction canst thou have tonight?

Romeo: Th'exchange of thy love's faithful vow for mine.

Juliet: I gave thee mine before thou didst request it;
And yet I would it were to give again.

Romeo: Wouldst thou withdraw it? For what purpose, love?

Juliet: But to be frank and give it thee again.
And yet I wish but for the thing I have.
My bounty is as boundless as the sea,
My love as deep; the more I give to thee
The more I have, for both are infinite.
I hear some noise within; dear love adieu.

                            (**Nurse** *calls within*)

Anon good Nurse! Sweet Montague, be true.
Stay but a little, I will come again.

Romeo: O blessed, blessed night! I am afeard,
Being in night, all this is but a dream,
Too flattering-sweet to be substantial.

                            (*Enter* **Juliet** *again*)

Juliet: Three words, dear Romeo, and good night indeed.
If that thy bent of love be honourable,
Thy purpose marriage, send me word tomorrow,
By one that I'll procure to come to thee,
Where and what time thou wilt perform the rite;

	And all my fortunes at thy foot I'll lay,
	And follow thee my lord throughout the world.
Nurse:	(*Within*) Madam!
Juliet:	I come, anon – But if thou meanest not well,
	I do beseech thee-
Nurse:	(*Within*) Madam!
Juliet:	By and by, I come –
	To cease thy strife, and leave me to my grief.
	Tomorrow will I send.
Romeo:	So thrive my soul –
Juliet:	A thousand times good night. (*Exit*)
Romeo:	A thousand times the worse, to want thy light.

William Shakespeare

Much Ado About Nothing

In Extract E, from *Much Ado About Nothing*, we see Beatrice and Benedick expressing their love for one another in rather different terms. Claudio, a friend of Benedick, had fallen in love with Beatrice's cousin, Hero. Just before the wedding ceremony between Claudio and Hero, a servant in the pay of the wicked Don John supplies Claudio with apparently 'visual' proof of Hero's infidelity. Claudio denounces Hero in church and she collapses. The Friar advises that Hero should be reported dead in order to bring Claudio to repentance. In this scene, Beatrice and Benedick, who have long had verbal duels with each other, at last declare their love for one another.

Kenneth Branagh and Emma Thompson as Benedick and Beatrice

Act IV Scene 1

Benedick: Surely I do believe your fair cousin is wronged.

Beatrice: Ah, how much might the man deserve of me that would right her!

Benedick: Is there any way to show such friendship?

Beatrice: A very even way, but no such friend.

Benedick: May a man do it?

Beatrice: It is a man's office, but not yours.

Benedick: I do love nothing in the world so well as you; is not that strange?

Beatrice: As strange as the thing I know not. It were as possible for me to say I loved nothing so well as you; but believe me not, and yet I lie not; I confess nothing nor I deny nothing. I am sorry for my cousin.

Benedick: By my sword, Beatrice, thou lovest me.

Beatrice: Do not swear and eat it.

Benedick: I will swear by it that you love me; and I will make him eat it that says I love not you.

Beatrice: Will you not eat your word?

Benedick: With no sauce that can be devised to it; I protest I love thee.

Beatrice: Why, then, God forgive me!

Benedick: What offence, sweet Beatrice?

Beatrice: You have stayed me in a happy hour; I was about to protest I loved you.

Benedick: And do it with all thy heart.

Beatrice: I love you with so much of my heart that none is left to protest.

Benedick: Come, bid me do anything for thee.

Beatrice: Kill Claudio.

Benedick: Ha! Not for the wide world.

Beatrice: You kill me to deny it. Farewell.

Benedick: (*taking her by the hand*) Tarry, sweet Beatrice.

Beatrice: I am gone though I am here; there is no love in you. Nay, I pray you, let me go.

Benedick: Beatrice –

Beatrice: In faith, I will go.

Benedick: We'll be friends first.

Beatrice: You dare easier be friends with me than fight with mine enemy.

Benedick: Is Claudio thine enemy?

Beatrice: Is he not approved in the height a villain that hath slandered, scorned, dishonoured my kinswoman? O that I were a man! What, bear her in hand until they come to take hands, and then, with public accusation, uncovered slander, unmitigated rancour – God, that I were a man! I would eat his heart in the market-place.

Benedick: Hear me, Beatrice –

Beatrice: Talk with a man out at a window! A proper saying!

Benedick:	Nay, but Beatrice –
Beatrice:	Sweet Hero! She is wronged, she is slandered, she is undone.
Benedick:	Beat –
Beatrice:	Princes and counties! Surely, a princely testimony, a goodly count, Count Comfect; a sweet gallant, surely! O that I were a man for his sake, or that I had any friend would be a man for my sake! But manhood is melted into curtsies, valour into compliment, and men are only turned into tongue, and trim ones too. He is now as valiant as Hercules that only tells a lie and swears it. I cannot be a man with wishing, therefore I will die a woman with grieving.
Benedick:	Tarry, good Beatrice. By this hand, I love thee.
Beatrice:	Use it for my love some other way than swearing by it.
Benedick:	Think you in your soul the Count Claudio hath wronged Hero?
Beatrice:	Yea, as sure as I have a thought or a soul.
Benedick:	Enough, I am engaged; I will challenge him. I will kiss your hand, and so I leave you. By this hand, Claudio shall render me a dear account. As you hear of me, so think of me. Go, comfort your cousin; I must say she is dead; and so, farewell.

(Exeunt)

William Shakespeare

ACTIVITY

1 Read both extracts carefully.
2 What view of love do Romeo and Juliet have? Do you detect any differences between them?
3 Compare the images that Romeo and Juliet use to express their feelings at this point.
4 What worries Juliet about Romeo's attitude?
5 What does Juliet say about the way she wants Romeo to speak of his love?
6 How does the way in which Beatrice and Benedick talk of their love differ from Romeo and Juliet's?
7 What kind of imagery do they use to express their feelings?
8 Write an essay in which you compare and contrast the attitudes towards love and the way each character expresses his or her feelings in each extract.

Sons and Lovers

In this extract from D. H. Lawrence's novel *Sons and Lovers*, the main character, Paul Morel, ends a long-standing relationship with Miriam. He has long felt trapped by the relationship and realizes now that it lacks something fundamental, although Miriam does not see things in the same light.

It was nearly five o'clock when he told her. They were sitting on the bank of a stream, where the lip of turf hung over a hollow bank of yellow earth, and he was hacking away with a stick, as he did when he was perturbed and cruel.

'I have been thinking,' he said, 'we ought to break off.'

'Why?' she cried in surprise.

'Because it's no good going on.'

'Why is it no good?'

'It isn't. I don't want to marry. I don't want ever to marry. And if we're not going to marry, it's no good going on.'

'But why do you say this now?'

'Because I've made up my mind.'

'And what about these last months, and the things you told me then?'

'I can't help it; I don't want to go on.'

'You don't want any more of me?'

'I want us to break off – you be free of me, I free of you.'

'And what about these last months?'

'I don't know. I've not told you anything but what I thought was true.'

'Then why are you different now?'

'I'm not – I'm the same – only I know it's no good going on.'

'You haven't told me why it's no good.'

'Because I don't want to go on – and I don't want to marry.'

'How many times have you offered to marry me, and I wouldn't?'

'I know; but I want us to break off.'

There was silence for a moment or two, while he dug viciously at the earth. She bent her head, pondering. He was an unreasonable child. He was like an infant which, when it has drunk its fill, throws away and smashes the cup. She looked at him, feeling she could get hold of him and *wring* some consistency out of him. But she was helpless. Then she cried:

'I have said you were only fourteen – you are only *four*!'

He still dug at the earth viciously. He heard.

'You are a child of four,' she repeated in her anger.

He did not answer, but said in his heart: 'All right; if I'm a child of four, what do you want me for? *I* don't want another mother.' But he said nothing to her, and there was silence.

'And have you told your people?' she asked.

'I have told my mother.'

There was another long interval of silence.

'Then what do you *want*?' she asked.

'Why, I want us to separate. We have lived on each other all these years; now let us stop. I will go my own way without you, and you will go your way without me. You will have an independent life of your own then.'

There was in it some truth that, in spite of her bitterness, she could not help registering. He knew she felt in a sort of bondage to him, which she hated because she could not control it. She had hated her love for him from the moment it grew too strong for her. And, deep down, she had hated him because she loved him and he dominated her. She had resisted his domination. She had fought to keep herself free of him in the last issue. And she *was* free of him, even more than he of her.

'And,' he continued, 'we shall always be more or less each other's work. You have done a lot for me, I for you. Now let us start and live by ourselves.'

'What do you want me to do?' she asked.

'Nothing – only be free,' he answered.

. . . She bit her finger moodily. She thought over their whole affair. She had known it would come to this; she had seen it all along. It chimed with her bitter expectation.

'Always – it has always been so!' she cried. 'It has been one long battle between us – you fighting away from me.'

It came from her unawares, like a flash of lightning. The man's heart stood still. Was this how she saw it?

'But we've had *some* perfect hours, *some* perfect times, when we were together!' he pleaded.

'Never!' she cried; 'never! It has always been you fighting me off.'

'Not always – not at first!' he pleaded.

'Always, from the very beginning – always the same!'

She had finished, but she had done enough. He sat aghast. He had wanted to say, 'It has been good, but it is at an end.' And she – she whose love he had believed in when he had despised himself – denied that their love had ever been love.

D. H. Lawrence

ACTIVITY

1 In this extract the 'action' of the piece takes place predominantly through dialogue between Paul and Miriam. Make a plan of the way in which the dialogue is patterned or structured between the two characters.
2 What differences in attitude do you detect between the two characters?
3 Sum up the feelings of a) Paul and b) Miriam. Do they change throughout the piece?
4 How does Lawrence's description, placed between the elements of dialogue, add to your understanding of what is going on in the characters' minds?
5 What does Lawrence mean when he says, 'She had finished, but she had done enough'?
6 Sum up your thoughts on the style in which this piece is written.

Earlier in this unit we looked at poems that give a fairly bleak picture of love and reflect on relationships that for one reason or another are at an end. It does seem that poems about the break-up of love are much more common than those which extol its joys. In the next group of poems, however, we see a broader range of attitudes towards love. Also in this section you will find an extract from Richard Sheridan's *The Rivals*.

Shall I Compare Thee To A Summer's Day?

Shall I compare thee to a summer's day?
Thou art more lovely and more temperate:
Rough winds do shake the darling buds of May,
And summer's lease hath all too short a date:
Sometime too hot the eye of heaven shines,
And often is his gold complexion dimmed;
And every fair from sometime declines,
By chance or nature's changing course untrimmed;
But thy eternal summer shall not fade,
Nor lose possession of that fair thou owest;
Nor shall Death brag thou wander'st in his shade,
When in eternal lines to time thou growest:
    So long as men can breathe, or eyes can see,
    So long lives this, and this gives life to thee.

William Shakespeare

Love Songs in Age

She kept her songs, they took so little space,
    The covers pleased her:
One bleached from lying in a sunny place,
One marked in circles by a vase of water,
One mended, when a tidy fit had seized her,
    And coloured, by her daughter –
So they had waited, till widowhood
She found them, looking for something else, and stood

Relearning how each frank submissive chord
    Had ushered in
Word after sprawling hyphenated word,
And the unfailing sense of being young
Spread out like a spring-woken tree, wherein
    That hidden freshness snug,
That certainty of time laid up in store
As when she played them first. But, even more,

The glare of that much-mentioned brilliance, love,
    Broke out, to show

Its bright incipience sailing above,
Still promising to solve, and satisfy,
And set unchangeably in order. So
    To pile them back, to cry
Was hard, without lamely admitting how
It had not done so then, and could not now.

Philip Larkin

Sonnet from the Portuguese XLIII

How do I love thee? Let me count the ways.
I love thee to the depth and breadth and height
My soul can reach, when feeling out of sight
For the ends of Being and ideal Grace.
I love thee to the level of every day's
Most quiet need, by sun and candlelight.
I love thee freely, as men strive for Right;
I love thee purely, as they turn from Praise.
I love thee with the passion put to use
In my old griefs, and with my childhood's faith.
I love thee with a love I seemed to lose
With my lost saints, – I love thee with the breath,
Smiles, tears, of all my life! – and, if God choose,
I shall but love thee better after death.

Elizabeth Barrett Browning

The Good-Morrow

I wonder by my troth, what thou, and I
Did, till we lov'd? were we not wean'd till then?
But suck'd on countrey pleasures, childishly?
Or snorted we i'the seaven sleepers den?
'Twas so; But this, all pleasures fancies bee.
If ever any beauty I did see,
Which I desir'd, and got, t'was but a dreame of thee.

And now good morrow to our waking soules,
Which watch not one another out of feare;
For love, all love of other sights controules,

And makes one little roome, an every where.
Let sea-discoverers to new worlds have gone,
Let Maps to other, worlds on worlds have showne,
Let us possesse one world, each hath one, and is one.

My face in thine eye, thine in mine appears,
And true plaine hearts doe in the faces rest,
Where can we finde two better hemispheares
Without sharpe North, without declining West?
What ever dyes, was not mixed equally;
If our two loves be one, or, thou and I
Love so alike, that none doe slacken, none can die.

John Donne

Love's Philosophy

The fountains mingle with the river
And the rivers with the ocean,
The winds of heaven mix for ever
With a sweet emotion;
Nothing in the world is single,
All things by a law divine
In one another's being mingle –
Why not I with thine?

See the mountains kiss high heaven
And the waves clasp one another;
No sister-flower would be forgiven
If it disdain'd its brother;
And the sunlight clasps the earth,
And the moonbeams kiss the sea –
What are all these kissings worth,
If thou kiss not me?

Percy Bysshe Shelley

The Rivals

This extract is taken from *The Rivals*, by Richard Sheridan, which was first written and presented on stage in 1777. The hero, Captain Absolute, has been wooing a beautiful young woman, Lydia, who has very romantic notions of love. She wants to experience the romance of falling in love with a penniless young officer, eloping to be secretly married against the will of her guardian and aunt, Mrs Malaprop. Here she finds that the penniless young subaltern she thought she was in love with is, in fact, the wealthy officer Captain Absolute. She realizes that what lies in store for her is a conventional marriage to a wealthy young man who has the full approval of her aunt.

Act IV Scene 2

Absolute:	What, Lydia, now that we are as happy in our friends' consent, as in our mutual vows –
Lydia:	(*Peevishly*) Friends' consent, indeed!
Absolute:	Come, come, we must lay aside some of our romance – a little wealth and comfort may be endured after all. And for your fortune, the lawyers shall make such settlements as –
Lydia:	Lawyers! I *hate* lawyers!
Absolute:	Nay then, we will not wait for their lingering forms, but instantly procure the licence, and –
Lydia:	The licence! I *hate* licence!
Absolute:	O my love! Be not so unkind! – thus let me entreat (*kneeling*)
Lydia:	Pshaw! – what signifies kneeling, when you know I *must* have you?
Absolute:	(*Rising*) Nay, Madam, there shall be no constraint upon your inclinations, I promise you. If I have lost your *heart* – I resign the rest. (*Aside*) Gad, I must try what a little *spirit* will do.
Lydia:	(*Rising*) Then, Sir, let me tell you, the interest you had there was acquired by a mean, unmanly imposition, and deserves the punishment of fraud. What, you have been treating *me* like a *child*! – humouring my romance! and laughing, I suppose, at your success!
Absolute:	You wrong me, Lydia, you wrong me – only hear –
Lydia:	(*Walking about in heat*) So, while I fondly imagined we were deceiving my relations, and flattered myself that I should outwit and incense them all – behold! my hopes are to be crushed at once, by my aunt's consent and approbation! – and I am myself the only dupe at last!
Absolute:	Nay, but hear me –
Lydia:	No, Sir, you could not think that such a paltry artifices could please me, when the mask was thrown off! But I suppose since your tricks have made you secure of my fortune, you are little solicitous about my affections. – But here, Sir, here is the picture – Beverley's picture! (*Taking a miniature from her bosom*) which I have worn, night and day, in spite of threats and entreaties! There, Sir, (*Flings it to him*) and be assured I throw the original from my heart as easily!
Absolute:	Nay, nay, Ma'am, we will not differ as to that. Here, (*Taking out a picture*) here is Miss Lydia Languish. What a difference! – aye,

there is the heavenly assenting smile, that first gave soul and spirit to my hopes! – those are the lips which sealed a vow, as yet scarce dry in Cupid's calendar! – and there, the half resentful blush, that would have checked the ardour of my thanks. – Well, all that's past! – all over indeed! There, Madam – in beauty, that copy is not equal to you, but in my mind its merit over the original, in being still the same, is such – that – I cannot find in my heart to part with it. (*Puts it up again*)

Lydia: (*Softening*) 'Tis your own doing, sir – I, I, I suppose you are perfectly satisfied.

Absolute: Oh, most certainly – sure now this is much better than being in love! – ha! ha! ha! – there's some spirit in *this*! What signifies breaking some scores of solemn promises – all that's of no consequence you know. To be sure people will say, that Miss didn't know her own mind – but never mind that: or perhaps they may be ill-natured enough to hint, that the gentleman grew tired of the lady and forsook her – but don't let that fret you.

Lydia: There's no bearing his insolence. (*Bursts into tears*)

Richard Sheridan

ACTIVITY

1   Basing your answer on **two** of the poems G–K, write a comparison of the ways in which your chosen writers present their ideas on, and attitudes towards, love. You should focus closely on each poet's use of language, form and structure in your answer.

2   Choose **one** poem that you have not discussed in question 1 and, by comparing your chosen poem with extract L, examine the style and treatment of the subject of love in these writings. You should consider:
    • language, form and structure
    • the character's or writer's attitude towards love
    • your own evaluation of the effectiveness of each piece of writing.

The Literature of Love:

Further activities

1   Choosing any two or three extracts as a starting point, examine the different ways in which writers of different periods choose to present ideas of love. Refer also to your own wider reading if it is relevant.

2   Collect your own extracts from literature based on the theme of love and make notes on the key aspects of each one.

3   Do any of the texts you have studied during your course deal with the idea of love? If so, make notes on the ways in which each writer chooses to present love, and the attitudes that are shown towards it. Select some passages or extracts from the text to illustrate your ideas.

5

Childhood in Literature

Children have qualities which writers appreciate: newly arrived in the world, they see it without the complications of adult experience, thought and association; their imaginations are less hampered by convention and they may be able to feel things with an intensity lost later in life; also, they may have fewer inhibitions and express themselves with a directness unthinkable for those who have 'grown up'. When writers portray children in fiction or drama, explore their own earliest memories in autobiographical writing, or reflect on childhood in poetry, they are usually trying to capture something of this refreshing approach.

A 'romantic' view of childhood such as this is particularly associated with Wordsworth, who believed that poets – and adults in general – had much to learn from children. He articulated the view that it is necessary to be in touch with a childlike way of experiencing the world in order to write imaginatively – and to live happily:

My heart leaps up when I behold
  A rainbow in the sky
So was it when my life began;
So is it now I am a man;
So be it when I shall grow old
  Or let me die!
The Child is father of the Man . . .

These are not the only possible responses to the characteristics of childhood, of course. In other times, such as the more strait-laced Victorian era, childlike behaviour was discouraged and children were expected to be 'seen and not heard'. Also, intense childhood experiences may be full of pain or humiliation rather than delight, and while some writers may present children as little angels, others, like William Golding in *Lord of the Flies*, suggest that they might also be little devils, or at least that they are ordinary mortals with feet of clay.

Literature about childhood varies with factors like time, place, culture or the age and gender of the writer. Although there are no particular rules, there are a few preliminary questions you might want to consider when you encounter texts like these.

- What is the writer's **viewpoint**? Does the writing attempt to explore the experience of childhood from the inside, or through memory, or does it portray childhood from the outside – the perspective of an adult bystander or witness? (This may or may not correspond to the use of first- or third-person narrative.)

- Does the writing reveal any particular **attitude** to children and childhood, or does it **challenge** such conventional attitudes?
- Is it possible to see this writing in relation to the **beliefs** or **cultural context** of the time and place in which it is set or written?
- Does the fact that childhood is the subject matter affect the way in which the writer uses **language**? For example, does the writer choose simpler vocabulary or syntax to convey a child's perceptions.

Macbeth

Discussing the children who appear in Shakespeare's plays, one critic calls them 'Shakespeare's boys' – for young girls do not feature. The boys usually fulfil small roles but can be important for what they add in terms of pathos and dramatic irony. One example is the dialogue between Richard and his nephews, the 'princes in the tower', in *Richard III*.

The following is an extract from Act IV of *Macbeth*. Now King of Scotland after murdering his predecessor Duncan, Macbeth is insecure and feels compelled to get rid of anyone who may suspect his crime or threaten his sovereignty. The witches, who initially predicted his rise to power, warn him that Macduff poses such a threat, but Macduff has already fled to England to gather forces to fight Macbeth. In desperation, Macbeth orders an attack on Macduff's wife and children. Here we see Lady Macduff and her young son in the moments before their murderers arrive. Lady Macduff is talking with her relative Ross about the flight of Macduff.

Act IV Scene 2

> *Enter **Lady Macduff**, her **Son**, and **Ross**.*

Lady Macduff: What had he done to make him fly the land?

Ross: You must have patience, madam.

Lady Macduff: He had none.
His flight was madness; when our actions do not,
Our fears do make us traitors.

Ross: You know not
Whether it was his wisdom or his fear.

Lady Macduff: Wisdom! To leave his wife, to leave his babes,
His mansion and his titles, in a place
From whence himself does fly? He loves us not.
He wants the natural touch; for the poor wren,
The most diminutive of birds, will fight,

Her young ones in her nest, against the owl.
All is the fear and nothing is the love,
As little is the wisdom, where the flight
So runs against all reason.

Ross: My dearest coz,
I pray you school yourself. But for your husband,
He is noble, wise, judicious, and best knows
The fits o'the season. I dare not speak much further,
But cruel are the times when we are traitors
And do not know ourselves; when we hold rumour
From what we fear, yet know not what we fear,
But float upon a wild and violent sea,
Each way and none. I take my leave of you;
Shall not be long but I'll be here again.
Things at the worst will cease or else climb upward
To what they were before. – My pretty cousin,
Blessing upon you!

Lady Macduff: Fathered he is, and yet he's fatherless.

Ross: I am so much a fool, should I stay longer
It would be my disgrace and your discomfort.
I take my leave at once.   *Exit*

Lady Macduff: Sirrah, your father's dead.
And what will you do now? How will you live?

Son: As birds do, mother.

Lady Macduff: What, with worms and flies?

Son: With what I get, I mean; and so do they.

Lady Macduff: Poor bird, thou'dst never fear
The net nor lime, the pitfall nor the gin!

Son: Why should I, mother? Poor birds they are not set for.
My father is not dead, for all your saying.

Lady Macduff: Yes, he is dead. How wilt thou do for a father?

Son: Nay, how will you do for a husband?

Lady Macduff: Why, I can buy me twenty at any market.

Son: Then you'll buy 'em to sell again.

Lady Macduff: Thou speak'st with all thy wit;
And yet, i'faith, with wit enough for thee.

Son: Was my father a traitor, mother?

Lady Macduff: Ay, that he was.

Son: What is a traitor?

Lady Macduff: Why, one that swears and lies.

Son: And be all traitors that do so?

Lady Macduff: Every one that does so is a traitor,
And must be hanged.

Son: And must they all be hanged that swear and lie?

Lady Macduff: Every one.

Son: Who must hang them?

Lady Macduff: Why, the honest men.

Son:	Then the liars and swearers are fools; for there are liars and swearers enough to beat the honest men and hang up them.
Lady Macduff:	Now God help thee, poor monkey! But how wilt thou do for a father?
Son:	If he were dead, you'd weep for him; if you would not, it were a good sign that I should quickly have a new father.
Lady Macduff:	Poor prattler, how thou talk'st.
	Enter a **Messenger**
Messenger:	Bless you, fair dame! I am not to you known,
	Though in your state of honour I am perfect.
	I doubt some danger does approach you nearly.
	If you will take a homely man's advice,
	Be not found here. Hence with your little ones!
	To fright you thus methinks I am too savage;
	To do worse to you were fell cruelty,
	Which is too nigh your person. Heaven preserve you!
	I dare abide no longer. *Exit*
Lady Macduff:	Whither should I fly?
	I have done no harm. But I remember now
	I am in this earthly world, where to do harm
	Is often laudable, to do good sometime
	Accounted dangerous folly. Why then, alas,
	Do I put up that womanly defence
	To say I have done no harm?
	Enter **Murderers** What are these faces?
Murderer:	Where is your husband?
Lady Macduff:	I hope in no place so unsanctified
	Where such as thou mayst find him.
Murderer:	He's a traitor.
Son:	Thou liest, thou shag-haired villain!
Murderer:	What, you egg,
	Young fry of treachery!
	He stabs him
Son:	He has killed me, mother!
	Run away, I pray you.
	Son *dies. Exit* **Lady Macduff** *crying 'Murder'*

William Shakespeare

ACTIVITY

1 With a partner read and discuss the dialogue between Lady Macduff and her son. How would you describe the tone of the exchange? How would you expect an audience to respond to the mother and child here? In what ways might it affect our response to what follows?
2 Make notes on how Shakespeare portrays the young boy here. Look both at the son's own words and at the language with which other characters refer to him.

3 Write a short essay in which you examine the way this child is presented by Shakespeare. Is he a real 'character' or merely a device for generating irony and an emotional response from the audience? Consider the evidence for each of these views in your answer.

Anecdote for Fathers

Showing How the Practice of Lying May be Taught

As we saw above, the romantic view of the child as 'father of the Man' was important to William Wordsworth. This poem is from *Lyrical Ballads*, a collection published in 1805, in which he aims to write in a clear, simple style, using 'the real language of men', and includes, among his characters, poorer countryside dwellers, women, and children, who had rarely featured in poetry before. Here he relates an incident in which a father learns something important from his child.

I have a boy of five years old;
His face is fair and fresh to see;
His limbs are cast in beauty's mould,
And dearly he loves me.

One morn we strolled on our dry walk,
Our quiet home all full in view,
And held such intermitted talk
As we are wont to do.

My thoughts on former pleasures ran:
I thought of Kilve's delightful shore,
Our pleasant home, when spring began,
A long, long year before.

A day it was when I could bear
To think, and think, and think again;
With so much happiness to spare,
I could not feel a pain.

My boy was by my side, so slim
And graceful in his rustic dress!
And oftentimes I talked to him,
In very idleness.

The young lambs ran a pretty race;
The morning sun shone bright and warm;
'Kilve,' said I, 'was a pleasant place;
And so is Liswyn farm.

'My little boy, which like you more,'
I said, and took him by the arm –
'Our home by Kilve's delightful shore,
Or here at Liswyn farm?'

'And tell me, had you rather be,'
I said, and held him by the arm,
'At Kilve's smooth shore by the green sea,
Or here at Liswyn farm?'

In careless mood he looked at me,
While still I held him by the arm,
And said, 'At Kilve I'd rather be
Than here at Liswyn farm.'

'Now, little Edward, say why so;
My little Edward, tell me why.'
'I cannot tell, I do not know.'
'Why, this is strange,' said I.

'For here are woods, and green-hills warm:
There surely must some reason be
Why you would change sweet Liswyn farm
For Kilve by the green sea.'

At this, my boy hung down his head,
He blushed with shame, nor made reply;
And five times to the child I said,
'Why, Edward, tell me why?'

His head he raised: there was in sight –
It caught his eye, he saw it plain –
Upon the house-top, glittering bright,
A broad and gilded vane.

Then did the boy his tongue unlock;
And thus to me he made reply:
'At Kilve there was no weather-cock,
And that's the reason why.'

O dearest, dearest boy! My heart
For better lore would seldom yearn,
Could I but teach the hundredth part
Of what from thee I learn.

William Wordsworth

ACTIVITY

1 Make notes on the language Wordsworth uses to describe the boy and the surroundings.
2 What *does* the father learn from his son? Discuss the points Wordsworth is making here about the difference in the ways adults and children respond to things.
3 Write a critical appreciation of the poem.

A Mother to her Waking Infant

Next, the Scottish Romantic poet Joanna Baillie (1762–1851) writes about her own – much younger – child in a rather different way.

Now in thy dazzled half-oped eye,
Thy curled nose and lip awry,
Uphoisted arms and noddling head,
And little chin with crystal spread,
Poor helpless thing! what do I see,
That I should sing of thee?

From thy poor tongue no accents come,
Which can but rub thy toothless gum:
Small understanding boasts thy face,
Thy shapeless limbs nor step nor grace:
A few short words thy feats may tell,
And yet I love thee well.

When wakes the sudden bitter shriek,
And redder swells thy little cheek
When rattled keys thy woes beguile,
And through thine eyelids gleams the smile,
Still for thy weakly self is spent
Thy little silly plaint.

But when thy friends are in distress,
Thou'lt laugh and chuckle n'ertheless,
Nor with kind sympathy be smitten,
Though all are sad but thee and kitten;
Yet puny varlet that thou art,
Thou twitchest at the heart.

Thy smooth round cheek so soft and warm;
Thy pinky hand and dimpled arm;
Thy silken locks that scantly peep,
With gold-tipped ends, where circles deep,
Around thy neck in harmless grace,
So soft and sleekly hold their place,
Might harder hearts with kindness fill,
And gain our right goodwill.

Each passing clown bestows his blessing,
Thy mouth is worn with old wives' kissing;
E'en lighter looks the gloomy eye
Of surly sense when thou art by;
And yet, I think, whoe'er they be,
They love thee not like me.

Perhaps when time shall add a few
Short months to thee, thou'lt love me too;
And after that, through life's long way,
Become my sure and cheering stay;
Wilt care for me and be my hold,
When I am weak and old.

Thou'lt listen to my lengthened tale,
And pity me when I am frail –
But see, the sweepy spinning fly
Upon the window takes thine eye.
Go to thy little senseless play;
Thou dost not heed my lay.

Joanna Baillie

ACTIVITY

1 Discuss the points Baillie is making about babies and about the mother–child relationship. How would you describe her tone of voice in her words to the child? What feelings does she reveal?
2 Make notes on the language and structure of the poem.
3 Write a detailed commentary on the poem, focusing on the way Baillie presents the relationship between the mother and her child.

Silas Marner

George Eliot's novel *Silas Marner* was published in 1861, but it presents a picture of rural life at the beginning of the nineteenth century. It is an allegory with a moral. Marner, wrongly accused of theft and betrayed by his friends, has left his former home and religious community to live as a lonely, miserly weaver, his attention devoted only to work and the accumulation of gold. When his precious money is stolen, he finds in its place a small orphaned child. Through caring for her, he learns once more to appreciate the human values of love and trust.

Unlike the gold which needed nothing, and must be worshipped in close-locked solitude – which was hidden away from the daylight, was deaf to the song of birds, and started to no human tones – Eppie was a creature of endless claims and ever-growing desires, seeking and loving sunshine, and living sounds, and living movements; making trial of everything, with trust in new joy, and stirring the human kindness in all eyes that looked on her. The gold had kept his thoughts in an ever-repeated circle, leading to nothing beyond itself; but Eppie was an object compacted of changes and hopes that forced his thoughts onward, and carried them far away from their old eager pacing towards the same blank limit – carried them away to the new things that would come with the coming years, when Eppie would have learned to understand how her father Silas cared for her; and made him look for images of that time in the ties and charities that bound together the families of his neighbours. The gold had asked that he should sit weaving longer and longer, deafened and blinded more and more to all things except the monotony of his loom and the repetition of his web; but Eppie called him away from his weaving, and made him think all its pauses a holiday, reawakening his senses with her fresh life, even to the old winter-flies that came crawling forth in the early spring sunshine, and warming him into joy because *she* had joy.

And when the sunshine grew strong and lasting, so that the buttercups were thick in the meadows, Silas might be seen in the sunny mid-day, or in the late afternoon when the shadows were lengthening under the hedgerows, strolling out with uncovered head to carry Eppie beyond the Stone-pits to where the flowers grew, till they reached some favourite bank where he could sit down, while Eppie toddled to pluck the flowers, and make remarks to the winged things that murmured happily above the bright petals, calling 'Dad-dad's' attention continually by bringing him the flowers. Then she would turn her ear to some sudden bird-note, and Silas learned to please her by making signs of hushed stillness, that they might listen for the note to come again: so that when it came, she set up her small back and laughed with gurgling triumph. Sitting on the banks in this way, Silas began to look for the once familiar herbs again; and as the leaves, with their unchanged outline and markings, lay on his palm, there was a sense of crowding remembrances from which he turned away timidly, taking refuge in Eppie's little world, that lay lightly on his enfeebled spirit.

As the child's mind was growing into knowledge, his mind was growing into memory: as her life unfolded, his soul, long stupefied in a cold narrow prison, was unfolding too, and trembling gradually into full consciousness.

It was an influence which must gather force with every new year: the tones that stirred Silas's heart grew articulate, and called for more distinct answers; shapes and sounds grew clearer for Eppie's eyes and ears, and there was more that 'Dad-dad' was imperatively required to notice and account for.

George Eliot

ACTIVITY

1 Make notes on the language George Eliot uses to describe the child's effect on Marner.
2 Write in detail about how George Eliot presents the relationship between Silas Marner and the small child Eppie in this extract.

A Sketch of the Past

In the following extract, a modernist writer experiments with ways of recording her earliest memories in writing. Virginia Woolf wrote her *Sketch of the Past* in 1939 when her sister suggested that she would 'soon be too old' to write her memoirs and would forget these impressions of her childhood in the 1880s.

Virginia Woolf

I begin: the first memory.

This was of red and purple flowers on a black ground – my mother's dress; and she was sitting either in a train or in an omnibus, and I was on her lap. I therefore saw the flowers she was wearing very close; and can still see purple and red and blue, I think, against the black; they must have been anemones, I suppose. Perhaps we were going to St Ives; more probably, for from the light it must have been evening, we were coming back to London. But it is more convenient artistically to suppose that we were going to St Ives, for that will lead to my other memory, which also seems to be my first memory, and in fact it is the most important of all my memories. If life has a base that it stands upon, if it is a bowl that one fills and fills and fills – then my bowl without a doubt stands upon this memory. It is of lying half asleep, half awake, in bed in the nursery at St Ives. It is of hearing the waves breaking, one, two, one, two, and sending a splash of water over the beach; and then breaking, one, two, one, two, behind a yellow blind. It is of hearing the blind draw its little acorn across the floor as the wind blew the blind out. It is of lying and hearing this splash and seeing this light, and feeling, it is almost impossible that I should be here; of feeling the purest ecstasy I can conceive. . . .

But to fix my mind upon the nursery – it had a balcony; there was a partition, but it joined the balcony of my father's and mother's bedroom. My mother would come out onto her balcony in a white dressing gown. There were passion flowers growing on the wall; they were great starry blossoms, with purple streaks, and large green buds, part empty, part full.

If I were a painter I should paint these first impressions in pale yellow, silver, and green. There was the pale yellow blind; the green sea; and the silver of the passion flowers. I should make a picture that was globular; semi-transparent. I should make a picture of curved petals; of shells; of things that were semi-transparent. I should make curved shapes, showing the light through, but not giving a clear outline. Everything would be large and dim;

and what was seen would at the same time be heard; sounds would come through this petal or leaf – sounds indistinguishable from sights. Sound and sight seem to make equal parts of these first impressions. When I think of the early morning in bed I also hear the caw of rooks falling from a great height. The sound seems to fall through an elastic, gummy air; which holds it up; which prevents it from being sharp and distinct. The quality of the air above Talland House seemed to suspend sound, to let it sink down slowly, as if it were caught in a blue gummy veil. The rooks cawing is part of the waves breaking – one, two, one, two – and the splash as the wave drew back and then it gathered again, and I lay there half awake, half asleep, drawing in such ecstasy as I cannot describe.

The next memory – all these colour-and-sound memories hang together at St Ives – was much more robust; it was highly sensual. It was later. It still makes me feel warm; as if everything were ripe; humming; sunny; smelling so many smells at once; and all making a whole that even now makes me stop – as I stopped then going down to the beach; I stopped at the top to look down at the gardens. They were sunk beneath the road. The apples were on a level with one's head. The gardens gave off a murmur of bees; the apples were red and gold; there were also pink flowers and grey and silver leaves. The buzz, the croon, the smell, all seemed to press voluptuously against some membrane; not to burst it; but to hum round one such a complete rapture of pleasure that I stopped, smelt, looked. But again I cannot describe that rapture. It was rapture rather than ecstasy.

Virginia Woolf

ACTIVITY

1   Make notes on how Woolf approaches this exploration of her memories and feelings. What is her viewpoint? What do you notice about the way she uses colour, the senses, imagery and about the construction of her sentences?
2   Write a critical commentary on the passage.
3   Experiment with some different ways of writing about your own childhood memories.

The Little Girl's Room

Elizabeth Bowen (1899–1973) was born in Dublin but later lived in London. This extract is from a short story published in 1934.

This was Geraldine's moment. At a nod from Mrs Letherton-Channing, carefully guarding the flame of her taper, she passed round the circle from cigarette to cigarette. The little girl's serious movements, the pretty shell of her hand, the soft braids of hair as she stooped, swinging over her shoulders, the soft creak of her plaited sandals as she stepped, cast some kind of spell on the talk: silence followed her like a shadow.

At first Clara Ellis frowned: talk of a first-rate scandalous quality had been held up. But: 'Why,' she exclaimed, glancing at Geraldine's arm, 'you freckle just like a cowslip!'

'Do I?' blushed Geraldine.

They all said 'Dear thing'. . . or 'How good of you, Geraldine dear.'

General Littlecote ducked to the flame in her hands rather grimly, as though the pleasure were bitter. Smoke began to go up in the afternoon light of the room; the green-panelled drawing-room, with bowls of lush yellow roses, ornate with Florentine furniture: smoke wreathed out of the high open windows across the magnolia flowering unseen. Geraldine reached her step-grandmother's chair and politely waited.

'Mr Scutcheon is late,' said Mrs Letherton-Channing.

'He's come,' said Geraldine gently. 'I saw him come up through the garden.'

'Really,' exclaimed Mrs Letherton-Channing. 'How should he know the way?' Her face became expressionless with annoyance. For who knew how this might end? Indeed, it would never do to have professors of Greek and Latin, Italian and German masters, mathematicians, historians and even Swedish exponents of physical culture, finding their way through her garden at every hour. Meditation and intimate talk became imperilled. For Geraldine was being highly educated at home.

'Perhaps Miss Weeks showed him,' said Geraldine. 'Ought I to go?' she added.

'Why, certainly, if he *is* here,' snapped Mrs Letherton-Channing.

Mrs Letherton-Channing was a widow, with one step-son. The son's wife, Vivien, a difficult and rather derisive step-daughter-in-law, having died four years ago, the elder Mrs Letherton-Channing thereby succeeded to what she was determined to prove a wonder-child. Vivien had once kept her Geraldine very much to herself, but nowadays, Mrs Letherton-Channing, in the strong position of being alive, could speak generously of her daughter-in-law . . .

Geraldine, fostered in this atmosphere, was tempted in all directions to be exceptional. Each young tendril put out found a wire waiting; she clung and blossomed, while, ambushed in gentleness, Mrs Letherton-Channing watched like a lynx for the most tentative emanations of young genius. Geraldine was certainly *something*. In preparation for her apotheosis she found herself very much guarded, very much educated, very much petted. There was sometimes a touch of reverence in her step-grandmother's manner. Though the child still danced with anxious clumsiness, sang with a false little clear voice, was listless behind the pencil, nerveless upon the keyboard, heavy upon the bow; her small intellectual flame stooped and wavered; she was docile, but incurious . . . while, in fact, at twelve she could still only claim the divine attribute through that shining vague look and constant abstention from effort in any direction. Nobody was encouraged to contradict Geraldine: it became penal to hurt her feelings. The Beautiful, in all possible concrete forms, was placed about for her contemplation, till life, for her wilful fancy, became an obstacle race.

Mrs Letherton-Channing's afternoon visitors – old friends, aware of all this – were relieved on the whole when Geraldine left the room. Talk resumed its usual tenor of indiscretion. The child's presence had been like a flower put down in irrelevant purity alongside one's place at dinner, disconcerting to appetite. 'But what,' murmured a new-comer, a pretty foolish young mother, to Miss Ellis, 'does that poor little creature *do* with herself all day?'

Miss Ellis supposed that the child went into abeyance.

'But has she no governess?'

'Dear me, no: how prosaic!' exclaimed Miss Ellis. The child was no more to her at the moment than a thin little freckled arm.

Geraldine did not go immediately to the library where Mr Scutcheon, who had come out from Reading to instruct her in Greek, sat biting his nails. Waiting quietly in the hall, she intercepted another slice of the chocolate cake as it was carried out by the butler. She went down the garden: when she had finished her cake and licked her fingers she pulled a rose to pieces, plucking off even the stamens. She eyed the calyx with an obscure sensation of triumph, but had no thoughts. She made gargoyle faces; wishing that she could see herself, she ran to the pool, but the water was clotted with lily-leaves.

'Old Miss Ellis,' she said aloud, '*pink as hell is. General Littlecote . . . laughs like a little goat. Lady Miriam Glover . . . hops about like a plover.*' After reflection she added: '*That can't sit on her eggs . . . because of her long legs . . . Geraldine Letherton-Channing . . . ran in and ran in and ran in.*' Then she did run in, judging that Mr Scutcheon should by now have come to the boil and be cross enough.

Elizabeth Bowen

1 Discuss how Bowen presents Geraldine's experience of childhood here. What narrative viewpoint does she adopt? How would you describe her attitude to the adults in the story and to Geraldine herself? How is this reflected in the tone of her writing?

2 Make detailed notes on Bowen's use of language in the descriptions, action and dialogue.

3 Write in detail about the presentation of Geraldine in the extract.

We Remember Your Childhood Well

This poem, by the contemporary poet Carol Ann Duffy, is from a collection published in 1990.

Nobody hurt you. Nobody turned off the light and argued
with somebody else all night. The bad man on the moors
was only a movie you saw. Nobody locked the door.

Your questions were answered fully. No. That didn't occur.
You couldn't sing anyway, cared less. The moment's a blur, a
   Film Fun
laughing itself to death in the coal fire. Anyone's guess.

Nobody forced you. You wanted to go that day. Begged. You
   chose
the dress. Here are the pictures, look at you. Look at us all,
smiling and waving, younger. The whole thing is inside your
   head.

What you recall are impressions; we have the facts. We called
   the tune.
The secret police of your childhood were older and wiser than
   you, bigger
than you. Call back the sound of their voices. Boom. Boom.
   Boom.

Nobody sent you away. That was an extra holiday, with people
you seemed to like. They were firm, there was nothing to fear.
There was none but yourself to blame if it ended in tears.

What does it matter now? No, no, nobody left the skidmarks
   of sin
on your soul and laid you wide open for Hell. You were loved.
Always. We did what was best. We remember your childhood
   well.

Carol Ann Duffy

Note:

Film Fun: a comic containing cartoon strips of comedy films.

ACTIVITY   Write a critical appreciation of the poem.

Childhood in Literature:

Further activities

1   Choose three extracts to write about in detail, comparing and contrasting the ways in which different writers present children. You should consider
      • language, form and structure
      • the ways the writers use their chosen genres to express their thoughts and feelings
      • the writers' attitudes to children
      • the influence of the time at which the texts were written
      • the gender of the writers.

2 H. G. Wells described Joyce's *A Portrait of the Artist as a Young Man* as a 'living and convincing picture of an Irish Catholic upbringing'. Referring to any texts which interest you, discuss how far you find these 'pictures' of childhood 'living and convincing'.

3 Have attitudes to childhood and children changed with the passage of time? Referring to extracts from different eras and/or to your own wider reading, explore the similarities and differences you have encountered.

4 Do children see things differently from adults? Assess the evidence in two or three of the texts which focus on the relationships between adults and children. Refer also to your own wider reading, if it is relevant.

Student response

Here is one student's response to question 4 above. Compare it with your own work. How successful is her answer? Discuss it and/or make notes on its strengths and weaknesses.

> *Two texts which show children see things differently from adults are the poems 'Anecdote for Fathers' by Wordsworth and 'We Remember your Childhood Well' by Carol Ann Duffy.*
>
> *In Wordsworth's poem the narrator is enjoying spending time with his little boy in the countryside. It is obvious that the father loves his child as he tells us that:*
>
> > *His face is fair and fresh to see*
> > *His limbs are cast in beauty's mould*
>
> *and says that he is so happy being with his son that 'I could not feel a pain'. He also declares that the little boy loves him: 'dearly he loves me'.*
>
> *He describes the 'pleasant' countryside where 'the young lambs ran a pretty race' and 'the morning sun shone bright and warm'. However, in the third stanza, we are told that the father's mind is not really on what he is doing. Instead he is thinking about the past:*
>
> > *My thoughts on former pleasures ran:*
> > *I thought of Kilve's delightful shore*
> > *Our pleasant home, when spring began*
> > *A long, long year before.*
>
> *and comparing it with the present. This is something adults do more than children, who live more in the present moment. Without really thinking, 'oftentimes I talked to him/in very idleness', the father asks the boy whether he would rather be where they are now, Liswyn Farm, or back at Kilve, and the boy seems to answer without thinking much either – he's 'In careless mood'. He says he'd rather be at Kilve.*
>
> *At that point, the father's manner seems to change and he begins to demand that the boy should provide a 'reason' for his answer. Already*

Wordsworth has told us twice that he 'held him by the arm', which sounds as if he has to hold him physically to hold his attention to the question. The boy is young and has just said what he felt on the spur of the moment and doesn't really have a reason for his answer, but his father will not accept this: 'There surely must some reason be', he says, and puts more and more pressure on him:

> *Five times to the child I said,*
> *'Why, Edward, tell me why?'*

At last in desperation the boy looks around and uses the first thing he sees as an excuse for his answer: 'At Kilve there was no weathercock.' The father realizes that he has forced his son to tell a lie.

The poem shows that one difference between the way the adult and the child see things is that the child reacts more simply and just says what he feels, while the adult thinks about things much more, comparing the present with the past. Adults don't always trust their feelings, but want reasons and explanations. It also shows that the little boy wants to please his father. He blushes 'with shame' when he can't answer the question and tells the lie to get his father's approval.

Another reason for this is that the father is bigger and stronger than his child and he can hold him 'by the arm' and force him to answer, changing what he thinks to fit in with what the adult wants him to say.

This is true in Duffy's poem too. She also writes with the voice of a parent or parents, but this time directly to the child, who is now older. The child seems to be remembering some of the difficult and frightening experiences of childhood and the times when her parents may have let her down and is asking about them, but her parents 'remember' things differently and tell her that

> *What you recall are impressions; we have the facts. We called the tune.*

The poem shows that a child's memories may not always be clear cut and may be affected by what other people say about the past. They also see or remember things in different ways from the adults. For example, the child remembers being 'sent away', but the parents say 'That was an extra holiday.' They deny the child's perceptions and feelings, 'there was nothing to fear', and refuse to accept any blame, putting the blame on the child herself. 'There was none but yourself to blame if it ended in tears'. The parents in the poem need to believe that they 'did what was best' and deny her memories of bad experiences:

> *Nobody hurt you. Nobody turned off the light and argued*
> *With somebody else all night*

but because of the way this is written, the parents give themselves away. Some of the things they say 'didn't occur' are too specific for the child to have invented them. There are some sinister double meanings or suggestions in what they say. For example the people she was sent to stay with were 'firm', which might suggest harsh or even violent, and 'The whole thing is inside your head' sounds almost as if they are accusing her of being mad. It could also mean that the whole poem, and all the things her parents say, are 'inside her head' so that she now says these things to herself as well as hearing them from her parents. The parents also refer to themselves as 'the secret police of your childhood' suggesting that their actions were repressive and perhaps even cruel.

Like the father in Wordsworth's poem who interrogates his son, forcing him to answer, these 'police' were 'bigger than you' and their voices boomed. However, in Wordsworth's poem, the father is sorry when he realizes that he has done something wrong and admits that he cannot

> teach the hundredth part
> Of what from thee I learn.

The parents in Duffy's poem have to believe that they are right. They are complacent that their version of their child's past is the correct one:

> 'We remember your childhood well.'

Both poems show children seeing things in a different way from adults but present their ideas in contrasting ways. Wordsworth presents his incident quite simply and honestly, in a loving tone, as the father learns his lesson about honesty from his son, but Duffy's poem has a bitter ironic tone as she shows the parents refuse to acknowledge their child's point of view.

Heather

Examiner's comments

- This is quite a perceptive answer which draws attention to some interesting links and comparisons between two very different poems, although the student makes no reference to the different contexts in which the poems were written.
- She takes a little while to get into her stride – the first few paragraphs on Wordsworth tend towards being descriptive rather than analytical.
- The essay shows evidence of independent thought, although one or two of her ideas need to be explained more fully. For example, when writing about Duffy's poem, she suggests that 'the whole poem is inside her head'. This sounds interesting but she has not really made the implications clear.
- The student makes good use of quotations from the text and they are usually – but not always – incorporated neatly into her writing. In places the detailed analysis of particular words and phrases could be extended. There are some interesting lines in the Duffy poem, in the second and last stanzas, for example, which receive no comment at all.
- Ideas are expressed clearly and in an interesting way. Overall, this is promising work.

6

The Social Observer

Writers have always been interested in the kind of society within which they live and over the ages many have highlighted the problems, foibles of behaviour, inequalities, hypocrisies and injustices that have existed, and do exist, in the worlds we create for ourselves. Many have used their writings to argue for social change and reform, or at least to try to bring particular problems to readers' notice. Of course, the subjects highlighted by the writer as social observer can be varied and can range from the trivial to the serious. Here are some aspects of society that writers have focused on over the centuries:

- the plight of the poor or working class, and the effects of poverty
- the position of women in society
- injustices of various kinds
- working conditions in mills, etc.
- inequalities relating to class
- inequalities relating to race or gender
- the effects of the industrial revolution
- the need for a social revolution.

These are just some of the social issues that writers might focus on, and clearly it is important to consider the context here. Any writer's social observation or criticism obviously relates to the kind of society that existed at the time he or she was writing and so, to some extent at least, the work needs to be assessed in its social context. This is the case when you are assessing the content of the writing but need not necessarily be relevant when looking at the writer's style and the effectiveness of his or her use of language. You should also bear in mind that although a piece of literature may be rooted within the context in which it was produced, it may also have a wider relevance so that its context includes the society of today. Were this not the case, then the works of Shakespeare, for example, would be of no relevance to a modern audience.

You will be able to identify many of these issues in the poems and extracts that follow.

ACTIVITY Read the following poems (A, B and C) carefully. They were all written by William Blake (1757–1827).

1 Make notes on what Blake is saying in each of them.
2 Is there a common link between them as regards content?
3 Compare the ways in which Blake puts across his message in each of the poems. Which do you find most effective, and why? You should consider the following aspects of each poem:
   - structure
   - form – including rhyme and rhythm pattern
   - language use – including imagery and other figurative language
4 Think about the poems in terms of the historical period in which they were written. Does this context give them any added significance?
5 Do you think that the messages they hold have any significance to us today?

London

I wander thro' each charter'd street
Near where the charter'd Thames does flow,
And mark in every face I meet
Marks of weakness, marks of woe.

In every cry of every Man,
In every Infant's cry of fear,
In every voice, in every ban,
The mind-forg'd manacles I hear:

How the Chimney-sweeper's cry
Every black'ning Church appalls;
And the hapless Soldier's sigh
Runs in blood down Palace walls.

But most thro' midnight street to hear
How the youthful Harlot's curse
Blasts the new born Infant's tear,
And blights with plagues the Marriage hearse.

William Blake

A Little Boy Lost

'Nought loves another so,
Nor venerates another so,
Nor is it possible to Thought
A greater that itself to know:

'And father, how can I love you
Or any of my brothers more?
I love you like the little bird
That picks up crumbs around the door.'

The Priest sat by and heard the child,
In trembling zeal he seiz'd his hair:
He led him by his little coat,
And all admir'd the Priestly care.

And standing on the altar high,
'Lo, what a fiend is here!' said he,
'One who sets reason up for judge
Of our most holy Mystery.'

The weeping child could not be heard,
The weeping parents wept in vain;
They strip'd him to his little shirt,
And bound him in an iron chain;

And burn'd him in a holy place,
Where many had been burn'd before:
The weeping parents wept in vain.
Are such things done on Albion's shore?

William Blake

I Asked a Thief

I asked a thief to steal me a peach:
He turned up his eyes.
I asked a lithe lady to lie her down:
Holy and meek, she cries –

As soon as I went
An angel came.
He wink'd at the thief
And smil'd at the dame.

And without one word said
Had a peach from the tree,
And still as a maid
Enjoy'd the lady.

William Blake

Here are some ideas that you might have noted:

- In *London* the first stanza sets a depressing scene – Blake does not see one optimistic sign in all of London. In the second stanza everyone he meets is distressed and in the third, social injustice is revealed as the source of the problem.
- The injustice ranges from military conscription to forced child labour. According to Blake such misery often starts from birth, with births that are unwelcome.
- The language of the poem is one of unrelieved misery, focusing on injustice, oppression, vice and irresponsibility.
- In *A Little Boy Lost*, Blake raises questions. In the first stanza Blake proposes that nothing can love anything more than it loves itself. The boy can only love his parents in a limited way and this is taken as a kind of blasphemy.
- *I Asked a Thief* deals with the idea of the hypocrisy of those with power.

The following two poems present us with contrasting views of two very different societies. These two poems, *The Song of the Banana Man* and *The Lament of the Banana Man*, are by the Jamaican-born writer Evan Jones. He has written these poems in such a way as to try to capture the distinctive Caribbean voice of the Banana Man.

The Song of the Banana Man

Touris, white man, wipin his face,
Met me in Golden Grove market place.
He looked at m'ol' clothes brown wid stain,
An soaked right through wid de Portlan rain,
He cas his eye, turn up his nose,
He says, 'You're a beggar man, I suppose?'
He says, 'Boy, get some occupation,
Be of some value to your nation.'
   I said, 'By God and dis big right han
   You mus recognise a banana man.

'Up in de hills, where de streams are cool,
An mullet an janga swim in de pool,
I have ten acres of mountain side,
An a dainty-foot donkey dat I ride,
Four Gros Mitchel, and four Lacatan,
Some coconut trees, and some hills of yam,
An I pasture on dat very same lan

Five she-goats and a big black ram,
 Dat, by God an dis big right han
 Is de property of a banana man.

'I leave m'yard early-mornin time
An set m'foot to de mountain climb,
I ben m'back to de hot-sun toil,
An m'cutlass rings on de stony soil,
Ploughin an weedin, diggin and plantin
Till Massa Sun drop back o John Crow mountain,
Den home again in cool evenin time,
Perhaps whistling dis likkle rhyme,
 (*Sung*) Praise God an m'big right han
 I will live and die a banana man.

'Banana day is my special day,
I cut my stems and I'm on m'way,
Load up de donkey, leave de lan
Head down de hill to banana stan,
When de truck comes round I take a ride
All de way down to de harbour side –
Dat is de night, when you, touris man,
Would change your place wid a banana man.
 Yes, by God, an m'big right han
 I will live an die a banana man.

'De bay is calm, an de moon is bright
De hills look black for de sky is light,
Down at de dock is an English ship,
Restin after her ocean trip,
While on de pier is a monstrous hustle,
Tallymen, carriers, all in a bustle,
Wid stems on deir heads in a long black snake
Some singin de songs dat banana men make,
 Like, (*Sung*) Praise God an m'big right han
 I will live an die a banana man.

'Den de payment comes, an we have some fun,
Me, Zekiel, Breda and Duppy Son.
Down at de bar near United Wharf
We knock back a white rum, bus a laugh,
Fill de empty bag for further toil
Wid saltfish, breadfruit, coconut oil.
Den head back home to m'yard to sleep,
A proper sleep dat is long an deep.
 Yes, by God, an m'big right han
 I will live an die a banana man.

'So when you see dese ol clothes brown wid stain,
An soaked right through wid de Portlan rain,

Don't cas your eye nor turn your nose,
Don't judge a man by his patchy clothes,
I'm a strong man, a proud man, an I'm free,
Free as dese mountains, free as dis sea,
I know myself, an I know my ways,
An will sing wid pride to de end o my days
   (*Sung*) Praise God an m'big right han
   I will live an die a banana man.'

Evan Jones

Notes:

Golden Grove:	a small town in Eastern Jamaica which used to be a favourite spot for tourists to visit.
Portlan(d):	a few miles to the north of Golden Grove, mostly mountain land populated by small farmers. Banana growers would bring their crops down from the hills to the small ports where they would be picked up by the banana boats.
janga:	a crayfish.
Gros Mitchel, Lacatan:	varieties of banana.

The Lament of the Banana Man

Gal, I'm tellin you, I'm tired fro true,
Tired of Englan, tired o you.
But I can't go back to Jamaica now . . .

I'm here in Englan, I'm drawin pay,
I go to de underground every day –
Eight hours is all, half-hour fo lunch,
M' uniform's free, an m' ticket punch –
Punchin tickets not hard to do,
When I'm tired o punchin, I let dem through.

I get a paid holiday once a year.
Ol age an sickness can't touch me here.
I have a room of m' own, an a iron bed,
Dunlopillo under m' head,
A Morphy-Richards to warm de air,
A formica table, an easy chair.
I have summer clothes, an winter clothes,
An paper kerchiefs to bow m'nose.

My yoke is easy, my burden is light,
I know a place I can go to, any night.
Dis place Englan! I'm not complainin,
If it col', it col', if it rainin, it rainin.
I don't mind if it's mostly night,
Dere's always inside, or de sodium light.
I don't mind white people starin at me,
Dey don' want me here? Don't is deir country?
You won' catch me bawlin any homesick tears,
If I don' see Jamaica for a t'ousan years!

. . . Gal, I'm tellin you, I'm tired fo true,
Tired of Englan, tired o you,
I can't go back to Jamaica now –
But I'd want to die there, anyhow.

Evan Jones

ACTIVITY

1 There is a stark contrast between the Banana Man's existence in the two environments. Make notes on these differences.
2 How is he treated differently in the two societies?
3 Look carefully at the ways in which Jones uses language in each poem. What differences do you note?
4 Write an essay showing how Jones presents the nature of the Banana Man's experiences in his own country, compared with his experiences in England. You should refer closely to the poet's use of language and the effects he creates through it in both poems.

Student response

Here are the notes that one student made in response to questions 1, 2 and 3 above, in preparation for writing the essay:

> *1.*
>
> *There are several striking differences between the Banana Man's lifestyle and existence in the two environments. These being:*
>
> * *Self-perception In Jamaica he is seen to take pride in himself and his job – even suggesting that he has an envied existence. He also sees himself as being 'free', even though he has to work hard to earn a living. In England, although he has a lighter workload, his lack of pride shows in how he 'cuts corners' whilst doing his work: 'Punchin tickets not hard to do, / when I'm tired o punchin, I let dem through'.*
> * *Clothes The differences in the two environments appear to be symbolically represented in the clothes he wears. In Jamaica, his apparent 'freedom' is reflected in him wearing old, stained clothes – being proud that they mark him out as a Banana Man and therefore someone who works extremely hard. In England, his apparent 'restrictiveness' of*

existence is marked by him wearing a 'uniform' – moreover, unlike the old, stained clothes he was proud to wear in Jamaica, this uniform is given 'free' and therefore he is denied a sense of pride in wearing it.

- **Occupation** His occupation as a Banana Man in Jamaica can be seen to be somewhat fulfilling for him. He appears to be proud of his limited possessions, knowing that he has had to work extremely hard to acquire them. However, this sense of pride in his work is absent from his job on the Underground, as he seems to have to do very little in contrast for much 'apparent' reward: 'Eight hours is all,', 'I get a paid holiday once a year'.

- **Physical environment** In Jamaica we see the Banana Man working hard in the open air, being both appreciative of and a part of his natural environment. However, in stark contrast, in England he is working in the man-made environment of the Underground. This also reflects the apparent restrictiveness/freedom of the two different environments.

- **Possessions** The Banana Man's possessions also appear to be symbolic of the two differing environments. In Jamaica, he owns land and animals; things which reflect a natural, unadulterated image. However, in England, his possessions reflect the materialistic nature of a 'developed' society. This is evident in the brand names incorporated in the poem.

- **Social Life** In Jamaica we see how the Banana Man enjoys a social life, drinking with friends. However, in his 'Lament' he appears to lead a solitary life – a life in an environment in which he is not made to feel welcome by the people around him.

- **Perception of existence** The fact that the poem about his life in Jamaica is referred to as a 'song' (something associated with celebration) suggests that he is happy and content. This contrasts markedly with the 'Lament' of his existence in England.

2.

In Jamaica, the Banana Man is seen to be accepted by his fellow-workers as they enjoy well-earned, 'fun', social times together. However, his encounter with the white 'Touris' reveals how he is regarded by 'outsiders'. Because of his raggy, stained clothes, the tourist takes him to be a beggar and is quite condescending and disrespectful to him when he states: 'Boy, get some occupation, / Be of some value to your nation'. Evidence exists in the 'Lament' that the Banana Man is not welcome or respected by the people he meets in England. Here people 'stare' at him and their attitude towards him leads him to ask: 'Dey don' want me here? Don't is deir country?'

3.

In 'The Song of the Banana Man', Jones uses an abundance of natural imagery which aids in expressing the Banana Man's apparent state of 'freedom' and 'belonging' to his native Jamaica. These natural images are complemented by effective adjectives which reflect the Banana Man's affinity with, and appreciation of, his surroundings. For example, we read of 'a dainty-foot donkey', the 'hot-sun' and 'streams' which are 'cool', etc.

The everyday effort employed by the Banana Man, which is needed for him to earn a living, is reflected by the string of present continuous verb forms evident in the line: 'Ploughin and weedin, diggin and plantin'. This also succeeds is exposing the misconception of him being 'lazy' by the white tourist.

It is interesting to see the difference in language evident in the dialogue between the Banana Man and the tourist in Jamaica. The Banana Man's colloquial language, when responding to the tourist, stands in stark contrast to the tourist's Standard English accent. This technique successfully re-asserts the social 'gulf' between the two. In addition, the concluding two lines of each stanza almost acts as a chorus, thus re-enforcing the 'happy' state of the Banana Man through seeing the poem as a 'Song'.

In 'The Lament of the Banana Man', the language is quite different. We see the infiltration of brand names into the Banana man's vocabulary showing the impact upon him of a materialistic environment: 'Dunlopillo', 'Morphy-Richards'. In addition, the lengths of the stanzas themselves are all different, thus re-asserting the apparent discord of the Banana Man in these 'alien' surroundings.

In the 'Lament', Jones includes 'man-made' 'artificial' elements – these standing in stark contrast to the natural imagery of the 'Song' and re-enforcing the idea that the Banana Man's new existence is 'unnatural' for him. For instance, instead of the 'hot-sun' in the 'Song', we read of 'A Morphy-Richards to warm de air'.

In addition, in contrast to the present continuous verb forms evident in the 'Song' which present the Banana Man as being an 'actor' in his environment, Jones presents the Banana Man as being somewhat passive in his response to his new surroundings in England: 'if it col', it col', if it rainin, it rainin' – the repetition evoking a sense of monotony. The sense of monotony regarding his existence in England is further enhanced in the Lament's cyclical structure.

Sandra

Examiner's comments

1 The student has clearly examined both poems very closely and her notes reveal the level of detail that you need to think about in your own work. Notice how the notes range over a wide range of points and the student has elaborated on them, making some perceptive observations as she goes.

2 In question 2 the student offers a briefer response but nevertheless it is a succinct and relevant response which gets straight to the heart of the question.

3 Here again there is a detailed response identifying a range of relevant points, focusing on important areas such as the differences in language

used in the two poems and the effects that this creates. Reference to the effect of the cyclical structure here again reveals a perceptive mind at work.

Overall these notes show a very clear and perceptive preliminary response to the poem and form an excellent basis from which to move forward to write the full essay on these poems.

John Galsworthy (1867–1933) was a novelist and dramatist whose works were mainly published in the early part of the twentieth century. Many of his works commented on the social injustices of the time and one of his plays, *Justice* (produced in 1910), actually led directly to the reform of the practice of solitary confinement in prisons. His play *Strife* (produced in 1909) is about the effects of a strike at the Trenartha Tin Plate works. The play is set on the afternoon of February 7, and the strike has been going on all winter. In the following two extracts we see a speech by one of the strikers and another one by the Chairman of the company.

Strife (1)

In extract F, a Trade Union official, Simon Harness, has just tried to talk the men into reducing their demands in order to reach a settlement. Now Roberts, the men's leader, speaks to them.

Act II Scene 2

Roberts: Mr Simon Harness is a clever man, but he has come too late. (*With intense conviction.*) For all that Mr Simon Harness says, for all that Thomas, Rous, for all that any man present here can say – *We've won the fight!* (*The crowd sags nearer, looking eagerly up. With withering scorn.*) You've felt the pinch o't in your bellies. You've forgotten what that fight 'as been; many times I have told you; I will tell you now this once again. The fight o' the country's body and blood against a blood-sucker. The fight of those that spend theirselves with every blow they strike and every breath they draw, against a thing that fattens on them, and grows and grows by the law of *merciful* Nature. That thing is Capital!

A thing that buys the sweat o' men's brows, and the tortures o' their brains, at its own price. *Don't I* know that? Wasn't the work o' *my* brains bought for seven hundred pounds, and hasn't one hundred thousand pounds been gained them by that seven hundred without the stirring of a finger? It is a thing that will take as much and give you as little as it can. That's *Capital!* A thing that will say – 'I'm very sorry for you, poor fellows – you have a cruel time of it, I know,' but will not give one sixpence of its dividends to help you have a better time. That's Capital! Tell me, for all their talk is there one of them that will consent to another penny on the Income Tax to help the poor? That's Capital! A white-faced, stony-hearted monster! Ye have got it on its knees; are ye to give up at the last minute to save your miserable bodies pain ? When I went this morning to those old men from London, I looked into their very 'earts. One of them was sitting there – Mr Scantlebury, a mass of flesh nourished on us: sittin' there for all the world like the shareholders in this Company, that sit not moving tongue nor finger, takin' dividends – a great dumb ox that can only be roused when its food is threatened. I looked into his eyes and I saw *he was afraid –* afraid for himself and his dividends, afraid for his fees, afraid of the very shareholders he stands for; and all but one of them's afraid – like children that get into a wood at night, and start at every rustle of the leaves. I ask you, men – (*he pauses, holding out his hand till there is utter silence*) – Give me a free hand to tell them: 'Go you back to London. The men have nothing for you'. (*A murmuring.*) Give me that, an' I swear to you, within a week you shall have from London all you want.

Evans, Jago and others: A free hand! Give him a free hand! Bravo – bravo!

Roberts: 'Tis not for this little moment of time we're fighting (*the murmuring dies*) not for ourselves, our own little bodies, and their wants, 'tis for all those that come after throughout all time. (*With intense sadness.*) Oh! men – for the love o' them, don't roll up another stone upon their heads, don't help to blacken the sky, an' let the bitter sea in over them. They're welcome to the worst that can happen to me, to the worst that can happen to us all, aren't they – aren't they? If we can shake (*passionately*) that white-faced monster with the bloody lips, that has sucked the life out of ourselves, our wives and children, since the world began. (*Dropping the note of passion, but with the utmost weight and intensity*) If we have not the hearts of men to stand against it breast to breast, and eye to eye, and force it backward till it cry for mercy, it will go on sucking life; and we shall stay for ever what we are (*in almost a whisper*) less than the very dogs.

John Galsworthy

Strife (2)

In extract G, John Anthony, Chairman of The Trenartha Tin Plate works speaks to his directors.

Act III

Anthony: (*With a great sigh – slowly*) We have been made the subject of an attack. (*Looking round at* **Wilder** *and* **Scantlebury** *with ironical contempt.*) I take it on *my* shoulders. I am seventy-six years old. I have been Chairman of this Company since its inception two-and-thirty years ago. I have seen it pass through good and evil report. My connection with it began in the year that this young man was born. (**Edgar** *bows his head.* **Anthony** *gripping his chair, goes on.*) I have had to do with 'men' for fifty years; I've always stood up to them; I have never been beaten yet. I have fought the men of this Company four times, and four times I have beaten them. It has been said that I am not the man I was. (*He looks at* **Wilder**.) However that may be, I am man enough to stand to my guns.

(*His voice grows stronger. The double doors are opened.* **Enid** *slips in, followed by* **Underwood**, *who restrains her.*) The men have been treated justly, they have had fair wages, we have always been ready to listen to complaints. It has been said that times have changed; if they have, I have not changed with them. Neither will I. It has been said that masters and men are equal! Cant! There can only be one master in a house! Where two men meet the better man will rule. It has been said that Capital and Labour have the same interests. Cant! Their interests are as wide asunder as the poles. It has been said that the Board is only part of a machine. Cant! We *are* the machine; its brains and sinews; it is for us to lead and to determine what is to be done, and to do it without fear or favour. Fear of the men! Fear of the shareholders! Fear of our own shadows! Before I am like that, I hope to die. (*He pauses, and meeting his son's eyes, goes on.*) There is only one way of treating 'men' – with *the iron hand.* This half-and-half business, the half-and-half manners of this generation has brought all this upon us. Sentiment and softness, and what this young man, no doubt, would call his social policy. You can't eat cake and have it! This middle-class sentiment, or socialism, or whatever it may be, is rotten. Masters are masters, men are men! Yield one demand, and they will make it six. They are (*he smiles grimly*) like Oliver Twist, asking for more. If I were in *their* place I should be the same. But I am not in their place.

Mark my words: one fine morning, when you have given way here, and given way there – you will find you have parted with the ground beneath your feet, and are deep in the bog of bankruptcy; and with you, floundering in that bog, will be the very men you have given way to. I have been accused of being a domineering tyrant, thinking only of my pride – I am thinking of the future of this country, threatened with the black waters of confusion, threatened with mob government, threatened with what I cannot see. If by any conduct of mine I help to bring this on us, I shall be ashamed to look my fellows in the face.

John Galsworthy

ACTIVITY

1 Write a summary of the standpoint that a) Roberts, and b) Anthony adopt.
2 Make a list of the reasons that each give for taking the standpoint that they do.
3 Look carefully at the ways in which each speaker uses language:
   - Note down any words they use that you feel add weight and power to their argument.
   - Examine any examples of figurative language that either of them use, and evaluative its success as a way of persuading the audience.
   - Do either of the speakers use any rhetorical devices or techniques in order to add weight to their words? If so, what are they and how effective do you think they are?
   - Whose speech do you find most powerful, and why?

The conflict between employers and the employed, 'Labour versus Capital', and the relationship between the workers and those who employ them has been a central social issue for some writers. The following poem examines further the world of work and human toil, and has a view to express.

Song to the Men of England

Men of England, wherefore plough
For the lords who lay ye low?
Wherefore weave with toil and care
The rich robes your tyrants wear?

Wherefore feed, and clothe, and save,
From the cradle to the grave,
Those ungrateful drones who would
Drain your sweat – nay, drink your blood?

Wherefore, Bees of England, forge
Many a weapon, chain, and scourge,

That these stingless drones may spoil
The forced produce of your toil?

Have ye leisure, comfort, calm,
Shelter, food, love's gentle balm?
Or what is it ye buy so dear
With your pain and with your fear?

The seed ye sow, another reaps:
The wealth ye find, another keeps;
The robes ye weave, another wears;
The arms ye forge, another bears.

Sow seed, – but let no tyrant reap;
Find wealth, – let no impostor heap;
Weave robes, – let not the idle wear;
Forge arms, – in your defense you bear.

Shrink to your cellars, holes, and cells;
In halls ye deck another dwells.
Why shake the chains ye wrought? Ye see
The steel ye tempered glance on ye.

With plough and spade, and hoe and loom,
Trace your grave, and build your tomb,
And weave your winding-sheet, till fair
England be your sepulchre.

Percy Bysshe Shelley

ACTIVITY

1 Make notes on the views expressed by Shelley in this poem.
2 Are any of the ideas similar in any way to those expressed by either of the characters from *Strife* (extracts F and G)? If so, explain how.
3 Write an essay in which you discuss the ideas raised in the two extracts from *Strife* and the poem here. In your answer you should focus closely on the language each writer has used to achieve his effects.

The coming of the Industrial Revolution provoked a great deal of social change in a very short space of time. Ways of life that had gone on for centuries were transformed beyond all recognition within the space of a few years and, although the changes undoubtedly brought benefits, many people saw the damaging aspects of such rapid change. Two writers who observed at first hand the social changes brought about by industrialization, and recorded what they saw and what they felt about it in print, were Charles Dickens and later D. H. Lawrence. Following are two extracts from Lawrence's novel *The Rainbow* and one from Dickens's *Hard Times*.

The Rainbow (1)

He lived in a large new house of red brick, standing outside a mass of homogeneous red-brick dwellings, called Wiggiston. Wiggiston was only seven years old. It had been a hamlet of eleven houses on the edge of heathy, half-agricultural country. Then the great seam of coal had been opened. In a year Wiggiston appeared, a great mass of pinkish rows of thin, unreal dwellings of five rooms each. The streets were like visions of pure ugliness; a grey-black macadamized road, asphalt causeways, held in between a flat succession of wall, window, and door, a new-brick channel that began nowhere, and ended nowhere. Everything was amorphous, yet everything repeated itself endlessly. Only now and then, in one of the house-windows vegetables or small groceries were displayed for sale.

In the middle of the town was a large, open, shapeless space, or market-place, of black trodden earth, surrounded by the same flat material of dwellings, new red-brick becoming grimy, small oblong windows, and oblong doors, repeated endlessly, with just, at one corner, a great and gaudy public-house, and somewhere lost on one of the sides of the square, a large window opaque and darkish green, which was the post-office.

The place had the strange desolation of a ruin. Colliers hanging about in gangs and groups, or passing along the asphalt pavements heavily to work, seemed not like living people, but like spectres. The rigidity of the blank streets, the homogeneous amorphous sterility of the whole suggested death rather than life. There was no meeting place, no centre, no artery, no organic formation. There it lay, like the new foundation of a red-brick confusion rapidly spreading, like a skin-disease.

Just outside of this, on a little hill, was Tom Brangwen's big, red-brick house. It looked from the front upon the edge of the place, a meaningless squalor of ash-pits and closets and irregular rows of the backs of houses, each with its small activity made sordid by barren cohesion with the rest of the small activities. Farther off was the great colliery that went night and day. And all around was the country, green with two winding streams, ragged with gorse, and heath, the darker woods in the distance.

The whole place was just unreal, just unreal. Even now, when he had been there for two years, Tom Brangwen did not believe in the actuality of the place. It was like some gruesome dream, some ugly, dead, amorphous mood become concrete.

D. H. Lawrence

The Rainbow (2)

Ursula sat black-souled and very bitter, hearing the two of them talk. There seemed something ghoulish even in their very deploring the state of things. They seemed to take a ghoulish satisfaction in it. The pit was the great mistress. Ursula looked out of the window and saw the proud, demon-like colliery with her wheels twinkling in the heavens, the formless, squalid mass of the town lying aside. It was the squalid heap of side-shows. The pit was the main show, the *raison d'etre* of all.

How terrible it was! There *was* a horrible fascination in it – human bodies and lives subjected in slavery to that symmetric monster of the colliery. There was a swooning, perverse satisfaction in it. For a moment she was dizzy.

Then she recovered, felt herself in a great loneliness, wherein she was sad but free. She had departed. No more would she subscribe to the great colliery, to the great machine which has taken us all captives. In her soul, she was against it, she disowned even its power. It had only to be forsaken to be inane, meaningless. And she knew it was meaningless. But it needed a great, passionate effort of will on her part, seeing the colliery, still to maintain her knowledge that it was meaningless.

But her Uncle Tom and her mistress remained there among the horde, cynically reviling the monstrous state and yet adhering to it, like a man who reviles his mistress, yet who is in love with her. She knew her Uncle Tom perceived what was going on. But she knew moreover that in spite of his criticism and condemnation, he still wanted the great machine. His only happy moments, his only moments of pure freedom were he was serving the machine. Then, and then only, when the machine caught him up, was he free from the hatred of himself, could he act wholly, without cynicism and unreality.

His real mistress was the machine, and the real mistress of Winifred was the machine. She too, Winifred, worshipped the impure abstraction, the mechanisms of matter. There, there, in the machine, in service of the machine, was she free from the clog and degradation of human feeling. There, in the monstrous mechanism that held all matter, living or dead, in its service, did she achieve her consummation and her perfect unison, her immortality.

Hatred sprang up in Ursula's heart. If she could she would smash the machine. Her soul's action should be the smashing of the great machine. If she could destroy the colliery, and make all the men of Wiggiston out of work, she would do it. Let them starve and grub in the earth for roots, rather than serve such a Moloch as this.

D. H. Lawrence

Hard Times

Coketown, to which Messr Bounderby and Gradgrind now walked, was a triumph of fact; it had no greater taint of fancy in it than Mrs Gradgrind herself. Let us strike the key-note, Coketown, before pursuing our tune.

It was a town of red brick, or of brick that would have been red if the smoke and ashes had allowed it; but, as matters stood it was a town of unnatural red and black like the painted face of a savage. It was a town of machinery and tall chimneys, out of which interminable serpents of smoke trailed themselves for ever and ever, and never got uncoiled. It had a black canal in it, and a river that ran purple with ill-smelling dye, and vast piles of building full of windows where there was a rattling and a trembling all day long, and where the piston of the steam-engine worked monotonously up and down, like the head of an elephant in a state of melancholy madness. It contained several large streets all very like one another, and many small streets still more like one another, inhabited by people equally like one another, who all went in and out at the same hours, with the same sound upon the same pavements, to do the same work, and to whom every day was the same as yesterday and tomorrow, and every year the counterpart of the last and the next.

These attributes of Coketown were in the main inseparable from the work by which it was sustained; against them were to be set off, comforts of life which found their way all over the world, and elegancies of life which made, we will not ask how much of the fine lady, who could scarcely bear to hear the place mentioned. The rest of its features were voluntary, and they were these.

You saw nothing in Coketown but what was severely workful. If the members of a religious persuasion built a chapel there – as the members of eighteen religious persuasions had done – they made it a pious warehouse of red brick, with sometimes (but this only in highly ornamented examples) a bell in a bird-cage on the top of it. The solitary exception was the New Church; a stuccoed edifice with a square steeple over the door, terminating in four short pinnacles like florid wooden legs. All the public inscriptions in the town were painted alike, in severe characters of black and white. The jail might have been the infirmary, the infirmary might have been the jail, the town-hall might have been either, or both, or anything else, for anything that appeared to the contrary in the graces of their construction. Fact, fact, fact, everywhere in the material aspect of the town; fact, fact, fact, everywhere in the immaterial. The M'Choakumchild school was all fact, and the school of design was all fact, and the relations between master and man were all fact, and everything was fact between the lying-in hospital and the cemetery, and what you couldn't state in figures, or show to be purchaseable in the cheapest market and saleable in the dearest, was not, and never should be, world without end, Amen.

Charles Dickens

ACTIVITY

1 Choose one of the Lawrence extracts and compare his attitude to the social effects of industrial change with that presented by Dickens in his description of Coketown.

2 Bearing in mind that Dickens was writing in the nineteenth century and Lawrence in the twentieth, write an essay comparing and contrasting the ways in which each writer uses language in order to express his ideas in your selected extracts.

In the poem that follows, Matthew Arnold describes a tramp that he had seen in the streets of London. Almost a century later, George Orwell deliberately became a tramp in both Paris and London in order to find out for himself at first hand what it was like to live in that way. He recorded his experiences in his book *Down and Out in Paris and London* which was published in 1933. Extract M describes his experiences staying at one of London's 'spikes' (nightly accommodation for down and outs).

West London

Crouched on the pavement, close by Belgrave Square,
A tramp I saw, ill, moody, and tongue-tied.
A babe was in her arms, and at her side
A girl; their clothes were rags, their feet were bare.
Some labouring men, whose work lay somewhere there,
Passed opposite; she touched her girl, who hied
Across, and begged, and came back satisfied.
The rich she had let pass with frozen stare.
Thought I: 'Above her state this spirit towers;
She will not ask of aliens, but of friends,
Of sharers in a common human fate.
She turns from that cold succor, which attends
The unknown little from the unknown great,
And points us to a better time than ours.'

Matthew Arnold

Down and Out in Paris and London

The porter herded us all into the passage, and then told us to come into the bathroom six at a time, to be searched before bathing. The search was for money and tobacco, Romton being one of those spikes where you can smoke once you have smuggled your tobacco in, but it will be confiscated if it is found on you. The old hands had told us that the porter never searched below the knee, so before going in we had all hidden our tobacco in the ankles of our boots. Afterwards, while undressing, we slipped it into our coats, which we were allowed to keep, to serve as pillows.

The scene in the bathroom was extraordinarily repulsive. Fifty dirty, stark-naked men elbowing each other in a room twenty feet square, with only two bathtubs and two slimy roller towels between them all. I shall never forget the reek of dirty feet. Less than half the tramps actually bathed (I heard them saying that hot water is 'weakening' to the system), but they all washed their faces and feet, and the horrid greasy little clouts known as toe-rags which they bind round their toes. Fresh water was only allowed for men who were having a complete bath, so many men had to bathe in water where others had washed their feet. The porter shoved us to and fro, giving the rough side of his tongue when anyone wasted time. When my turn came for the bath, I asked if I might swill out the tub, which was streaked with dirt, before using it. He answered simply, 'Shut yer – mouth and get on with yer bath!' That set the social tone of the place, and I did not speak again.

When we had finished bathing, the porter tied our clothes in bundles and gave us workhouse shirts – grey cotton things of doubtful cleanliness, like abbreviated nightgowns. We were sent along to the cells at once, and presently the porter and the Tramp Major brought our supper across from the workhouse. Each man's ration was a half-pound wedge of bread smeared with margarine, and a pint of bitter sugarless cocoa in a tin billy. Sitting on the floor we wolfed this in five minutes, and at about seven o'clock the cell doors were locked on the outside, to remain locked till eight in the morning.

Each man was allowed to sleep with his mate, the cells being intended to hold two men apiece. I had no mate, and was put in with another solitary man, a thin scrubby-faced fellow with a slight squint. The cell measured eight feet by five by eight high, was made of stone, and had a tiny barred window high up in the wall and a spyhole in the door, just like a cell in a prison. In it were six blankets, a chamber-pot, a hot-water pipe, and nothing else whatever. I looked round the cell with a vague feeling that there was something missing. Then, with a shock of surprise, I realized what it was, and exclaimed:

'But I say, damn it, where are the beds?'

'*Beds?*' said the other man, surprised. 'There aren't no beds! What yer expect? This is one of them spikes where you sleeps on the floor. Christ! Ain't you got used to that yet?'

It appeared that no beds was quite a normal condition in the spike. We rolled up our coats and put them against the hot-water pipe, and made ourselves as comfortable as we could. It grew foully stuffy, but it was not warm enough to allow of our putting all the blankets underneath, so that we could only use one to soften the floor. We lay a foot apart, breathing into one another's face, with our naked limbs constantly touching, and rolling against one another whenever we fell asleep. One fidgeted from side to side, but it did not do much good; whichever way one turned there would be first a dull

George Orwell

numb feeling, then a sharp ache as the hardness of the floor wore through the blanket. One could sleep, but not for more than ten minutes on end.

About midnight the other man began making homosexual attempts on me – a nasty experience in a locked, pitch-dark cell. He was a feeble creature and I could manage him easily, but of course it was impossible to go to sleep again. For the rest of the night we stayed awake, smoking and talking. The man told me the story of his life – he was a fitter, out of work for three years. He said that his wife had promptly deserted him when he lost his job, and he had been so long away from women that he had almost forgotten what they were like. Homosexuality is general among tramps of long standing, he said.

At eight the porter came along the passage unlocking the doors and shouting 'All out!' The doors opened, letting out a stale, fetid stink. At once the passage was full of squalid, grey-shirted figures, each chamber-pot in hand, scrambling for the bathroom. It appeared that in the morning only one tub of water was allowed for the lot of us, and when I arrived twenty tramps had already washed their faces; I took one glance at the black scum floating on the water, and went unwashed. After this we were given a breakfast identical with the previous night's supper, our clothes were returned to us, and we were ordered out into the yard to work. The work was peeling potatoes for the paupers' dinner, but it was a mere formality, to keep us occupied until the doctor came to inspect us. Most of the tramps frankly idled. The doctor turned up at about ten o'clock and we were told to go back to our cells, strip and wait in the passage for the inspection.

Naked and shivering, we lined up in the passage. You cannot conceive what ruinous, degenerate curs we looked, standing there in the merciless morning light. A tramp's clothes are bad, but they conceal far worse things; to see him as he really is, unmitigated, you must see him naked. Flat feet, pot bellies, hollow chests, sagging muscles – every kind of physical rottenness was there. Nearly everyone was under-nourished, and some clearly diseased; two men were wearing trusses, and as for the old mummy-like creature of seventy-five, one wondered how he could possibly make his daily march.

Looking at our faces, unshaven and creased from the sleepless night, you would have thought that all of us were recovering from a week on the drink.

The inspection was designed merely to detect smallpox, and took no notice of our general condition. A young medical student, smoking a cigarette, walked rapidly along the line glancing us up and down, and not inquiring whether any man was well or ill. When my cell companion stripped I saw that his chest was covered with a red rash, and, having spent the night a few inches away from him, I fell into a panic about smallpox. The doctor, however, examined the rash and said that it was due merely to under-nourishment.

After the inspection we dressed and were sent into the yard, where the porter called our names over, gave us back any possessions we had left at the office, and distributed meal tickets. These were worth sixpence each, and were directed to coffee-shops on the route we had named the night before. It was interesting to see that quite a number of the tramps could not read, and had to apply to myself and other 'scholards' to decipher their tickets.

George Orwell

ACTIVITY   Choose whichever Lawrence passage you did not look at for the last activity (either I or J) and compare the ways in which language is used to express the writer's point of view here and in poem L and extract M.

The Social Observer:

Further activities

1   Think about the texts you have studied for your course or any other texts that you have read. Have any of them dealt with social themes, or has the writer made comments about the nature of society in any of them? If so make a note of them and how the writers have concerned themselves with society.

2   Choose any three of the extracts as a starting point to examine ways in which writers of different eras have written about the society they have seen around them.

3   Choose a particular writer who has written about aspects of society, and make a collection of extracts of his or her writings. Make notes on each piece you find.

7

Tragic Scenes

The genre of tragedy has obscure origins. It is not particularly helpful to know that the word 'tragedy' is derived from the Greek word meaning 'goat song'; no satisfactory explanation exists for the connection between the two. However, it is true that our modern idea of tragedy is likely to have developed from ancient rituals and through Greek drama, and it has been an important and lasting feature of literature since the earliest times. In its broadest sense, the tragic has always inspired writers, which is not surprising as by its very nature it provokes deep and powerful emotions within those who encounter it.

In literature, the term 'tragedy' is usually used to describe a play with an unhappy ending, although both poetry and prose can contain strong elements of tragedy and some could be called tragedies in their own right.

The best-known tragic dramas are those written by William Shakespeare. No doubt you have come across some of Shakespeare's tragedies during the course of your studies. The four that are usually considered his 'great' tragedies are *Hamlet*, *Macbeth*, *Othello* and *King Lear*. These are sometimes said to have certain common features, such as:

- the tragic hero is a person of power and influence
- he has a 'tragic flaw' or weakness that contributes to his downfall
- in the course of the play the hero moves from happiness to misery to death
- in the end, the hero comes to see and understand his own weakness
- emotions are usually purged at the end of the play (this is called *catharsis*) and the drama ends with a sense of peace and regeneration.

Some critics have found these views rather simplistic, however, and consider that they are not always true of all plays.

Othello

In the following extract Othello, who has been driven mad by jealousy as a result of Iago's scheming, has murdered his innocent wife, Desdemona. He had been taken in by Iago's cleverly worked strategy to make him believe Desdemona guilty of adultery. Here, Othello realizes the truth – that Desdemona was a true, loving and faithful wife to him.

ACTIVITY

1 What concerns Othello in the first part of the extract?
2 What do you make of Iago's response?
3 How do Lodovico and Cassio respond to a) Iago and b) Othello?
4 Examine Othello's final speech.
   • What does he have to say here?
   • How does he use language to enhance his message?
   • How does Shakespeare build up the tension in this extract, and how is the sense of tragedy intensified?
   • Compare Othello's final speech with the final speech of the hero or heroine of any other Shakespearian tragedy you have studied. You should compare the content, the language, the tone and mood created, and the effectiveness of each in bringing the play to its conclusion.

Act V Scene 2

Othello:	Will you, I pray, demand that demi-devil
	Why he hath thus ensnared my soul and body?
Iago:	Demand me nothing; what you know, you know:
	From this time forth I never will speak word.
Lodovico:	What! Not to pray?
Gratiano:	Torments will ope your lips.
Othello:	Well, thou dost best.
Lodovico:	Sir, you shall understand what hath befallen,
	Which, as I think, you know not. Here is a letter
	Found in the pocket of the slain Roderigo,
	And here another: the one of them imports
	The death of Cassio, to be undertook
	By Roderigo.
Othello:	O villain!
Cassio:	Most heathenish and most gross!
Lodovico:	Now here's another discontented paper
	Found in his pocket too; and this, it seems
	Roderigo meant to have sent this damned villain,
	But that, belike, Iago, in the nick,
	Came in and satisfied him.
Othello:	(*to* **Iago**) O thou pernicious caitiff!
	How came you, Cassio, by that handkerchief
	That was my wife's?
Cassio:	I found it in my chamber;
	And he himself confessed but even now
	That there he dropped it for a special purpose
	Which wrought to his desire.

Othello:	O fool, fool, fool!
Cassio:	There is besides, in Roderigo's letter,
	How he upbraids Iago, that he made him
	Brave me upon the watch, whereon it came
	That I was cast; and even but now he spake
	After long seeming dead – Iago hurt him,
	Iago set him on.
Lodovico:	(*to* **Othello**) You must forsake this room and go with us.
	Your power and your command is taken off
	And Cassio rules in Cyprus. For this slave,
	If there be any cunning cruelty
	That can torment him much, and hold him long,
	It shall be his. You shall close prisoner rest,
	Till that the nature of your fault be known
	To the Venetian state. Come, bring him away.
Othello:	Soft you; a word or two before you go.
	I have done the state some service and they know't
	No more of that. I pray you, in your letters
	When you shall these unlucky deeds relate,
	Speak of me as I am: nothing extenuate,
	Nor set down aught in malice. Then must you speak
	Of one that loved not wisely, but too well;
	Of one, not easily jealous but, being wrought,
	Perplexed in the extreme; of one whose hand,
	Like the base Indian, threw a pearl away
	Richer than all his tribe; of one whose subdued eyes,
	Albeit unused to the melting mood,
	Drop tears as fast as the Arabian trees
	Their med'cinable gum. Set you down this:
	And say, besides, that in Aleppo once
	Where a malignant and a turbaned Turk
	Beat a Venetian and traduced the state,
	I took by th'throat the circumcised dog
	And smote him thus.
	(*He stabs himself*)
Lodovico:	O bloody period!
Gratiano:	All that's spoke is marred!
Othello:	(*to* **Desdemona**) I kissed thee, ere I killed thee: no way but this,
	Killing myself, to die upon a kiss.
	(*He falls on the bed and dies*)
Cassio:	This did I fear, but thought he had no weapon,
	For he was great of heart.
Lodovico:	(*To* **Iago**) O, Spartan dog,
	More fell than anguish, hunger, or the sea,
	Look on the tragic loading of this bed:
	This is thy work. The object poisons sight:
	Let it be hid

(The curtains are drawn)

> Gratiano, keep the house
> And seize upon the fortunes of the Moor,
> For they succeed on you. (*To* **Cassio**) To you, Lord Governor,
> Remains the censure of this hellish villain:
> The time, the place, the torture, O, enforce it!
> Myself will straight aboard, and to the state
> This heavy act with heavy heart relate.   *(Exeunt)*

William Shakespeare

Here are some of the points that you might have focused on:

- In the first part of the scene Othello is concerned with *why* Iago has done this to him, and he is at a loss to understand it. He falls back on phrases like 'O villain' and 'O thou pernicious caitiff'. (Note the use of the 'O' here to express Othello's anguish.)
- Iago's refusal to speak adds to the sense of pointlessness and waste created by the murder of Desdemona. It also adds to our macabre fascination with what Iago has done and his motives (or lack of them) for doing it.
- Lodovico and Cassio deal with Iago in a brisk and definite way. Both Lodovico and Cassio show sympathy for Othello's plight and they reveal to him what has happened.
- Note the change in tone for Othello's final speech, and the richness of the imagery here. Think about the effects this creates.

Richard II

The series of short extracts that follow are from *The Tragedy of King Richard II*. This play deals with the fall of Richard, as he is forced to abdicate the throne in favour of his cousin Henry Bolingbroke, who becomes King Henry IV. Elizabethan audiences were accustomed to the doctrine of the Divine Right of Kings, which meant that a monarch was appointed by God. Clearly this is the view that Richard takes, and although it does not save him it does account for some of the imagery he uses to describe his own plight. The short extracts are taken from different points in the play, and show Richard reflecting on his own position.

Act IV Scene 1

Richard:
> And must I ravel out
> My weaved-up follies? Gentle Northumberland,
> If thy offences were upon record,
> Would it not shame thee in so fair a troop

To read a lecture of them? If thou wouldst,
There shouldst thou find one heinous article,
Containing the deposing of a king
And cracking the strong warrant of an oath,
Marked with a blot, damned in the book of heaven.
Nay, all of you that stand and look upon me,
Whilst that my wretchedness doth bait myself,
Though some of you – with Pilate – wash your hands,
Showing an outward pity, yet you Pilates
Have here delivered me to my sour cross,
And water cannot wash away your sin.

Act III Scene 2

Richard: Let's talk of graves, of worms, and epitaphs;
Make dust our paper, and with rainy eyes
Write sorrow on the bosom of the earth.
Let's choose executors and talk of wills –
And yet not so; for what can we bequeath
Save our deposèd bodies to the ground?
Our lands, our lives, and all are Bolingbroke's,
And nothing can we call our own but death
And that small model of the barren earth
Which serves as paste and cover to our bones.
For God's sake, let us sit upon the ground
And tell sad stories of the death of kings –
How some have been deposed, some slain in war,
Some haunted by the ghosts they have deposed,
Some poisoned by their wives, some sleeping killed,
All murdered. For within the hollow crown
That rounds the mortal temples of a king
Keeps Death his court; and there the antic sits,
Scoffing his state and grinning at his pomp,
Allowing him a breath, a little scene,
To monarchize, he feared, and kill with looks,
Infusing him with self and vain conceit,
As if this flesh which walls about our life
Were brass impregnable; and humoured thus,
Comes at the last, and with a little pin
Bores through his castle wall, and – farewell, king!

Act III Scene 3

Richard: What must the King do now? Must he submit?
The King shall do it. Must he be deposed?
The King shall be contented. Must he lose
The name of king? A God's name, let it go.
I'll give my jewels for a set of beads,

My gorgeous palace for a hermitage,
My gay apparel for an almsman's gown,
My figured goblets for a dish of wood,
My sceptre for a palmer's walking-staff,
My subjects for a pair of carvèd saints,
And my large kingdom for a little grave,
A little, little grave, an obscure grave;
Or I'll be buried in the King's highway,
Some way of common trade where subjects' feet
May hourly trample on their sovereign's head,
For on my heart they tread now whilst I live,
And buried once, why not upon my head?
Aumerle, though weepest, my tender-hearted cousin.
We'll make foul weather with despisèd tears.
Our sighs and they shall lodge the summer corn
And make a dearth in this revolting land.
Or shall we play the wantons with our woes,
And make some pretty match with shedding tears,
As thus to drop them still upon one place
Till they have fretted us a pair of graves
Within the earth, and therein laid?

Act IV Scene 1

(*Enter* **Richard** *and* **Duke of York**)

Richard: Alack, why am I sent for to a king
Before I have shook off the regal thoughts
Wherewith I reigned? I hardly yet have learned
To insinuate, flatter, bow, and bend my knee.
Give sorrow leave awhile to tutor me
To this submission. Yet I well remember
The favours of these men. Were they not mine?
Did they not sometime cry 'All hail!' to me?
So Judas did to Christ. But He in twelve
Found truth in all but one; I, in twelve thousand, none.
God save the King! Will no man say Amen?
Am I both priest and clerk? Well then, Amen.
God save the King, although I be not he;
And yet Amen, if Heaven do think him me.
To do what service am I sent for hither?

York: To do that office of thine own good will
Which tired majesty did make thee offer:
The resignation of thy state and crown
To Henry Bolingbroke.

Richard: Give me the crown.
(*To* **Bolingbroke**) Here, cousin – seize the crown. Here, cousin –
On this side, my hand; and on that side, thine.

Now is this golden crown like a deep well
That owes two buckets, filling one another,
The emptier ever dancing in the air,
The other down, unseen, and full of water.
That bucket down and full of tears am I,
Drinking my griefs, whilst you mount up on high.

William Shakespeare

Samuel West as Richard preparing to surrender his crown to Bolingbroke (David Troughton)

ACTIVITY

1 What view does Richard take of his own position? Think about:
   • the religious comparisons he uses.
   • the language he uses to describe his plight.
   • how he views those around him.
2 Choose a central character from a Shakespeare play you are studying or
   have studied, and collect three or four short extracts from the play that
   seem to you to be central to the way in which that character is presented.
   Examine the ways in which Shakespeare uses language to create the effects
   he wants on the audience.

Contemplations on death have always fascinated writers throughout the ages,
and dramatists, novelists and poets have explored the topic on all kinds of
levels. In the first two poems that follow, Dylan Thomas expresses his views
on death. The third poem is by Chidiock Tichborne who, in 1586, became
involved in the Babington Plot, a conspiracy to assassinate Queen Elizabeth
I. He was arrested, and hanged on 20 September. This poem was reputedly
written the night before his execution.

C

And Death Shall Have No Dominion

And death shall have no dominion.
Dead men naked they shall be one

With the man in the wind and the west moon;
When their bones are picked clean and the clean bones gone,
They shall have stars at elbow and foot;
Though they go mad they shall be sane,
Though they sink through the sea they shall rise again;
Though lovers be lost love shall not;
And death shall have no dominion.

And death shall have no dominion.
Under the windings of the sea
They lying long shall not die windily;
Twisting on racks when sinews give way,
Strapped to a wheel, yet they shall not break;
Faith in their hands shall snap in *two*,
And the unicorn evils run them through;
Split all ends up they shan't crack;
And death shall have no dominion.

And death shall have no dominion.
No more may gulls cry at their ears
Or waves break loud on the seashores;
Where blew a flower may a flower no more
Lift its head to the blows of the rain;
Though they be mad and dead as nails,
Heads of the characters hammer through daisies;
Break in the sun til the sun breaks down,
And death shall have no dominion.

Dylan Thomas

Do Not Go Gentle Into That Good Night

Do not go gentle into that good night,
Old age should burn and rave at close of day;
Rage, rage against the dying of the light.

Though wise men at their end know dark is right,
Because their words had forked no lightning they
Do not go gentle into that good night.

Good men, the last wave by, crying how bright
Their frail deeds might have danced in a green bay,
Rage, rage against the dying of the light.

Wild men who caught and sang the sun in flight,
And learn, too late, they grieved it on its way,
Do not go gentle into that good night.

Grave men, near death, who see with blinding sight
Blind eyes could blaze like meteors and be gay,
Rage, rage against the dying of the light.

And you, my father, there on the sad height,
Curse, bless, me now with your fierce tears, I pray.
Do not go gentle into that good night.
Rage, rage against the dying of the light.

Dylan Thomas

Elegy For Himself

Written in the Tower before His Execution, 1586

My prime of youth is but a frost of cares;
My feast of joy is but a dish of pain;
My crop of corn is but a field of tares;
And all my good is but vain hope of gain:
The day is past, and yet I saw no sun;
And now I live, and now my life is done.

My tale was heard, and yet it was not told;
My fruit is fall'n, and yet my leaves are green;
My youth is spent, and yet I am not old;
I saw the world, and yet I have not seen:
My thread is cut, and yet it is not spun;
And now I live and now my life is done.

I sought my death, and found it in my womb;
I looked for life, and saw it was a shade;
I trod the earth, and knew it was my tomb;
And now I die, and now I was but made;
My glass is full, and now my glass is run;
And now I live, and now my life is done.

Chidiock Tichborne

ACTIVITY

1 In the two poems by Thomas, compare and contrast the ways in which he handles the theme of death in each.
2 Which of Thomas's poems do you find the most effective?
3 How does Tichborne approach the theme of death in extract E?
4 Write an essay examining the poems in extracts C, D and E, comparing and contrasting what they each have to say about life and death. In your answer you should make detailed reference to the ways in which the poets use language to achieve their effects.

Jude the Obscure

Tragedy comes in many shapes and forms, but stories involving the death of children must be among the most heart-rending. In the following extract from *Jude the Obscure* by Thomas Hardy, the central character, Jude, and his cousin and 'common-law' wife, Sue, have to face the death of not just one but all three of their children.

'You must all come to this inn for a day or two,' he said. 'It is a rough place, and it will not be so nice for the children, but we shall have more time to look round. There are plenty of lodgings in the suburbs – in my old quarter of Beersheba. Have breakfast with me now you are here, my bird. You are sure you are well? There will be plenty of time to get back and prepare the children's meal before they wake. In fact, I'll go with you.'

She joined Jude in a hasty meal, and in a quarter of an hour they started together, resolving to clear out from Sue's too respectable lodging immediately. On reaching the place and going upstairs she found that all was quiet in the children's room, and called to the landlady in timorous tones to please bring up the tea-kettle and something for their breakfast. This was perfunctorily done, and producing a couple of eggs which she had brought with her she put them into the boiling kettle, and summoned Jude to watch them for the youngsters, while she went to call them, it being now about half-past eight o'clock.

Jude stood bending over the kettle, with his watch in his hand, timing the eggs so that his back was turned to the little inner chamber where the children lay. A shriek from Sue suddenly caused him to start round. He saw that the door of the room, or rather closet – which had seemed to go heavily upon its hinges as she pushed it back – was open, and that Sue had sunk to the floor just within it. Hastening forward to pick her up he turned his eyes to the little bed spread on the boards; no children were there. He looked in bewilderment round the room. At the back of the door were fixed two hooks for hanging garments, and from these the forms of the two youngest children were suspended, by a piece of box-cord round each of their necks, while from a nail a few yards off the body of little Jude was hanging in a similar manner. An overturned chair was near the elder boy, and his glazed eyes were slanted into the room; but those of the girl and the baby were closed.

Half paralyzed by the strange and consummate horror of the scene he let Sue lie, cut the cords with his pocket knife and threw the three children on the bed; but the feel of their bodies in the momentary handling seemed to say that they were dead. He caught up Sue, who was in fainting fits, and put her on the bed in the other room, after which he breathlessly summoned the landlady and ran out for a doctor.

When he got back Sue had come to herself, and the two helpless women, bending over the children in wild efforts to restore them, and the triplet of little corpses, formed a sight which overthrew self-command. The nearest surgeon came in, but, as Jude had inferred, his presence was superfluous. The children were past saving, for though their bodies were still barely cold it was conjectured that they had been hanging more than an hour. The probability held by the parents later, when they were able to reason on the case, was that the elder boy, on waking, looked into the outer room for Sue, and, finding her absent, was thrown into a fit of aggravated despondency that the events and information of the evening before had induced in his morbid temperament. Moreover a piece of paper was found upon the floor, on which was written, in the boy's hand, with the bit of lead pencil that he carried:

Done because we are too menny.

At sight of this Sue's nerves utterly gave way, an awful conviction that her discourse with the boy had been the main cause of the tragedy, throwing her into a convulsive agony which knew no abatement. They carried her away against her wish to a room on the lower floor; and there she lay, her slight figure shaken with her gasps, and her eyes staring at the ceiling, the woman of the house vainly trying to soothe her.

They could hear from this chamber the people moving about above, and she implored to be allowed to go back, and was only kept from doing so by the assurance that, if there were any hope, her presence might do harm, and the reminder that it was necessary to take care of herself lest she should endanger a coming life. Her inquiries were incessant, and at last Jude came down and told her there was no hope. As soon as she could speak she informed him what she had said to the boy, and how she thought herself the cause of this.

'No,' said Jude. 'It was in his nature to do it. The doctor says there are such boys springing up amongst us – boys of a sort unknown in the last generation – the outcome of new views of life. They seem to see all its terrors before they are old enough to have staying power to resist them. He says it is the beginning of the coming universal wish not to live. He's an advanced man, the doctor: but he can give no consolation to –'

Jude had kept back his own grief on account of her; but he now broke down; and this stimulated Sue to efforts of sympathy which in some degree distracted her from her poignant self-reproach. When everybody was gone, she was allowed to see the children.

The boy's face expressed the whole tale of their situation. On that little shape had converged all the inauspiciousness and shadow which had darkened the first union of Jude, and all the accidents, mistakes, fears, errors of the last. He was their nodal point, their focus, their expression in a single term. For the rashness of those parents he had groaned, for their ill-assortment he had quaked, and for the misfortunes of these he had died.

ACTIVITY

1 Write a summary of what happens in this passage.
2 How does Hardy present the scene?
3 Does he successfully evoke a sense of tragedy?
4 Examine the techniques that Hardy uses to create this sense of tragedy. Refer closely to his use of language.

War brings its own kind of tragedy and this has been a topic frequently written about by poets in many conflicts. In the poems that follow we see different responses to conflict. The first one is by a Second World War poet, Keith Douglas. In the second poem, Edwin Muir writes about a 'third world war' nuclear conflict and its aftermath.

Vergissmeinicht

Three weeks gone and the combatants gone,
returning over the nightmare ground
we found the place again, and found
the soldier sprawling in the sun.

The frowning barrel of his gun
overshadowing. As we came on
that day, he hit my tank with one
like the entry of a demon.

Look. Here in the gunpit spoil
the dishonoured picture of his girl
who has put: *Steffi. Vergissmeinicht*
in a copybook gothic script.

We see him almost with content
abased, and seeming to have paid
and mocked at by his own equipment
that's hard and good when he's decayed.

But she would weep to see today
how on his skin the swart flies move;
the dust upon the paper eye
and the burst stomach like a cave.

For here the lover and killer are mingled
who had one body and one heart.
And death who had the soldier singled
has done the lover mortal hurt.

Keith Douglas

The Horses

Barely a twelvemonth after
The seven days war that put the world to sleep,

Late in the evening the strange horses came.
By then we had made our covenant with silence,
But in the first few days it was so still
We listened to our breathing and were afraid.
On the second day
The radios failed; we turned the knobs; no answer.
On the third day a warship passed us, heading north,
Dead bodies piled on the deck. On the sixth day
A plane plunged over us into the sea. Thereafter
Nothing. The radios dumb;
And still they stand in corners of our kitchens,
And stand, perhaps, turned on, in a million rooms

All over the world. But now if they should speak,
If on a sudden they should speak again,
If on the stroke of noon a voice should speak,
We would not listen, we would not let it bring
That old bad world that swallowed its children quick
At one great gulp. We would not have it again.
Sometimes we think of the nations lying asleep,
Curled blindly in impenetrable sorrow,
And then the thought confounds us with its strangeness.
The tractors lie about our fields; at evening
They look like dank sea-monsters couched and waiting.
We leave them where they are and let them rust:
'They'll moulder away and be like other loam'.
We make our oxen drag our rusty ploughs,
Long laid aside. We have gone back
Far past our fathers' land.
                        And then, that evening
Late in the summer the strange horses came.
We heard a distant tapping on the road,
A deepening drumming; it stopped, went on again
And at the corner changed to hollow thunder.
We saw the heads
Like a wild wave charging and were afraid.
We had sold our horses in our fathers' time
To buy new tractors. Now they were strange to us
As fabulous steeds set on an ancient shield
Or illustrations in a book of knights.
We did not dare go near them. Yet they waited,
Stubborn and shy, as if they had been sent
By an old command to find our whereabouts
And that long-lost archaic companionship.
In the first moment we had never a thought
That they were creatures to be owned and used,
Among them were some half a dozen colts

Dropped in some wilderness of the broken world,
Yet new as if they had come from their own Eden.
Since then they have pulled our ploughs and borne our loads
But that free servitude still can pierce our hearts.
Our life is changed; their coming our beginning.

Edwin Muir

ACTIVITY

1 What is each poet saying about war?
2 Compare the ways in which each poet uses language to develop his ideas.
3 Write an essay comparing and contrasting these two poems, and saying which you find the most effective, and why.

The two poems that follow are about tragic road accidents and their aftermaths.

Auto Wreck

Its quick soft silver bell beating, beating,
And down the dark one ruby flare
Pulsing out red light like an artery,
The ambulance at top speed floating down
Past beacons and illuminated clocks
Wings in a heavy curve, dips down,
And brakes speed, entering the crowd.
The doors leap open, emptying light;
Stretchers are laid out, the mangled lifted
And stowed into the little hospital.
Then the bell, breaking the hush, tolls once,
And the ambulance with its terrible cargo
Rocking, slightly rocking, moves away,
As the doors, an afterthought, are closed.

We are deranged, walking among the cops
Who sweep glass and are large and composed.
One is still making notes under the light.
One with a bucket douches ponds of blood
Into the street and gutter.
One hangs lanterns on the wrecks that cling,
Empty husks of locusts, to iron poles.
Our throats were tight as tourniquets,
Our feet were bound with splints, but now,
Like convalescents intimate and gauche,
We speak through sickly smiles and warn
With the stubborn saw of common sense,

The grim joke and the banal resolution.
The traffic moves around with care,
But we remain, touching a wound
That opens to our richest horror.
Already old, the question
Who shall die? Becomes unspoken Who is innocent?
For death in war is done by hands;
Suicide has cause and stillbirth, logic;
And cancer, simple as a flower, blooms.
But this invites the occult mind,
Cancels our physics with a sneer,
And spatters all we knew of denouement
Across the expedient and wicked stones.

Karl Shapiro

Mid-term Break

I sat all morning in the college sick bay
Counting bells knelling classes to a close.
At two o'clock our neighbours drove me home.

In the porch I met my father crying –
He had always taken funerals in his stride –
And Big Jim Evans saying it was a hard blow.

The baby cooed and laughed and rocked the pram
When I came in, and I was embarrassed
By old men standing up to shake my hand

And tell me they were 'sorry for my trouble';
Whispers informed strangers I was the eldest,
Away at school, as my mother held my hand

In hers and coughed out angry tearless sighs.
At ten o'clock the ambulance arrived
With the corpse, stanched and bandaged by the nurses.

Next morning I went up into the room. Snowdrops
And candles soothed the bedside; I saw him
For the first time in six weeks. Paler now,

Wearing a poppy bruise on his left temple,
He lay in the four foot box as in his cot.
No gaudy scars, the bumper knocked him clear.

A four foot box, a foot for every year.

Seamus Heaney

ACTIVITY   Compare the ways in which each writer handles the subject matter. Comment
on the following areas in your answer:
- the ways in which language is used in each poem, including the effects
  of imagery
- the form chosen by each poet to express his ideas
- the structure of each poem, and how this contributes to the overall
  effect
- any other points about the poem that you find of interest.

Student response

Here is one student's response to this activity.

*Both poems, 'Mid-Term Break' and 'Auto Wreck' deal with the same subject
matter; that of road traffic accidents. In Seamus Heaney's poem, 'Mid-Term
Break', we read an account of the death of a four-year-old boy as told by
his elder brother. The structure of this poem, short, three-line stanzas,
appears to mimic the way that memory is recalled by short bursts of
'snapshot' images: '. . . I met my father crying – / He had always taken
funerals in his stride – / And Big Jim Evans saying it was a hard blow.'
Both the opening and closing two stanzas are complete and relate the poet's
memories before and after his brother's funeral. However, in contrast, the
central stanzas containing images of the funeral gathering are not complete
and are linked by enjambment. This technique succeeds in increasing the
pace of the poem, reflecting the poet's rush of painful memories which
culminate in the horrific image of: 'the corpse, stanched and bandaged'. The
two final lines of this poem make up a rhyming couplet and they succeed in
leaving the reader with a sense of finality.*

*The form and structure of Karl Shapiro's poem, 'Auto Wreck', is very
different from that of Heaney's rigid three-line stanzas. 'Auto Wreck' consists
of three stanzas of differing lengths, an approach which compliments the
poem's underlying theme of the 'unexpected': 'And spatters all we know of
denouement'. This idea is further enhanced by the poem being written in free
verse. Unlike Heaney, who appears to relate events without engaging with
them on an emotional level, Shapiro's three stanzas progress in their
reflection of events. The first stanza of this poem is a description of events
on the night of the accident and is followed by the poet's reaction to these
events in the second stanza. In the third and final stanza, the poet addresses
the reader directly thus encouraging a contemplation of events and a
personal response to them: 'Who shall die? . . . Who is innocent?'*

*Both poets succeed in using language effectively to express their ideas. In
Heaney's poem, the subject matter of 'death' is complimented by the way he
describes the school bell 'knelling'. Likewise, the bell of the ambulance in
Shapiro's poem 'tolls', both words having negative connotations and being*

associated with death. In 'Auto Wreck' there are many words and phrases which have clinical connotations and which succeed in supporting the subject matter. For example the ambulance's light is described as: 'Pulsing out red light like an artery', this appearing to be symbolic of the blood loss being experienced by the victim(s) of the accident. In addition, the poet describes his reactive state and his physical inertia by using clinical terminology: 'Our throats were tight as tourniquets, / Our feet were bound with splints'. The language used in this poem also enhances the disturbing nature of the subject matter. The bodies are 'mangled'; the wrecks are, 'Empty husks of locusts'; and the somewhat oxymoronic phrase, 'ponds of blood', serves us with contrasting images which succeed in increasing the disturbing nature of the poem.

Heaney's poem, too, contains language and contrasting images which disturb the reader. For example, while the funeral gathering is taking place the sense of grief is very much in evidence. However, in the midst of this extreme sadness: 'The baby cooed and laughed and rocked the pram'. Like Shapiro, Heaney uses an oxymoron to intensify the horror of the image he relates – the 'poppy bruise' on the dead boy's body. The word 'poppy' is particularly effective here. Not only is it an item associated with 'remembrance' and a word which conjures up an image of the colour and shape of the wound, but it is also a word you would expect a young child to use in his attempts to describe. Language is also used effectively by Heaney to contrast the emotionally charged environment of the funeral gathering with the comparative 'calm' of the morning after in the somewhat peaceful scene of the boy's body in the coffin: 'Snowdrops / And candles soothed the bedside.' Heaney's use of alliteration in the second line of the poem is an effective example of sound symbolism: 'Counting bells knelling classes to a close'. Alliterative technique is also evident in Shapiro's poem; the repetitive 's' sound being symbolic of the noise created by a saw: 'We speak through sickly smiles and warn / With the stubborn saw of common sense.'

In conclusion, both poets successfully use language to great effect in expressing their experiences of tragedy. The form and structure of each poem, although being different, succeed in reflecting the memories and ideas expressed.

Sandra

Examiner's comments

This is a fluent and tightly structured response, which includes a range of very perceptive and well-made points. The student successfully compares both poems and draws attention to the key difference in language, form and presentation. Notice the close attention paid to the language used in each poem – the student doesn't just quote lines, she really uses them to illustrate the points and explain what she means. Notice too, that although the student clearly has a sound knowledge of literary technical terms, not only does she know what they mean but she is able to describe the **effects** they create in the specific poems. This is vital in a good answer – it is not sufficient to simply say that there is some alliteration here or enjambment takes place there – the really important thing is to be able to recognize what effect they have on the overall impact of the poem.

Notice, too, this student's awareness of the differences in form between the two poems. Again she not only is able to describe the nature of these differences but she discusses how the form of each poem contributes to its effects.

Overall, this is a high quality response from a perceptive and able student.

The texts that follow are linked through their common theme of coal mining. Poem K is by Philip Larkin, and takes a pit explosion as its theme. Extract L is from a report by the journalist John Pilger describing his visit to a pit.

The Explosion

On the day of the explosion
Shadows pointed towards the pithead:
In the sun the slagheap slept.

Down the lane came men in pitboots
Coughing oath-edged talk and pipe-smoke,
Shouldering off the freshened silence.

One chased after rabbits; lost them;
Came back with a nest of lark's eggs;
Showed them; lodged them in the grasses.

So they passed in beards and moleskins,
Fathers, brothers, nicknames, laughter,
Through the tall gates standing open.

At noon, there came a tremor; cows
Stopped chewing for a second; sun,
Scarfed as in a heat-haze, dimmed.

The dead go on before us, they
Are sitting in God's house in comfort,
We shall see them face to face –

Plain as lettering in the chapels
It was said, and for a second
Wives saw men of the explosion

Larger than in life they managed –
Gold as on a coin, or walking
Somehow from the sun towards them,

One showing the eggs unbroken.

Philip Larkin

The Miners

It was approaching midnight at the pithead, and the first hand I took was a claw. 'It's me . . . Harry,' said its owner, knowing I had failed to recognise him. His hand, with three fingers gone and a stump, was no guide; so many hands were like that, which perhaps explained why so few were offered. 'Going into F32 are you?' said Harry. 'Aye, you'll know about pit down there.' At the bar of the Democratic Club the night before, F32 was the seam I was told to see; it lay a third of a mile beneath Murton and extended about four miles east, almost to the sea.

Harry's voice had filled the lamp room; except for brief, muttered monosyllables and the catching of breath, there was silence as we filled water bottles and strapped on rubber knee-pads and the 'self-rescuer', which is a small metal box with gas mask, designed to keep you alive until they reach you. We walked to the cage. We each carried two numbered metal tokens, one to hand to the banksman on the pithead as we went down and one to surrender when we came up. A missing token means a missing man. The banksman frisked us for matches and cigarettes and slammed shut the cage, which rocked with the freezing gale hitting the pithead at seventy miles an hour. There was total blackness now; no one spoke.

Just before one o'clock in the morning we reached 1,100 feet and the shift only now began; this was the time the Coal Board started paying. Now we were walking downhill through the swirls of stone dust, fudging the man in front from the beam of his lamp. Bill Williams, who had been doing this since he was fourteen, bit off some tobacco. 'Aye, that'll catch some of the muck,' he said. He also lifted his ribcage, as someone might hitch up his pants, and attempted to clear his lungs of 'the muck', but without success.

He made a sound I didn't take much notice of at first and which would reach a terrible crescendo later, in the pithead baths. It was a heaving from deep in the throat, followed by a stuttering wheeze and, finally, a hacking which went on for a minute or for a night, until the black phlegm was brought up. It was called 'the Dust', or pneumoconiosis. There were more than 40,000 registered sufferers of pneumoconiosis and thousands who were not registered, and there were countless others who died from diseases related to or caused by years of breathing in coal dust.

Now the atmosphere in the pit had changed. It was humid, almost tropical. The first mechanical sound was the hissing of the compression pumps, pumping out 200 gallons of water every minute. We were under old workings, which were flooded, and the roof was raining a steady drizzle of white slush, and the ground was silt. We were bent forward at right-angles, and my head slammed into a support. 'Look up, look down, lad,' said a voice from behind.

At two o'clock in the morning we reached the coal-face. Joe Canning and Doug Walton already wore masks of white clay as they worked a drill at the stone: the noise of the drill was incessant and the sting from the dust and water was relieved only when I lay on my stomach in the slush and crawled under the stone and into the tunnel beside the coal-face, which was three-and-a-half feet high and slightly wider than my shoulders. This was the core of the mine and, except for the machinery, it looked like a scene from a Victorian etching: the men, their bodies doubled, contorted, following the machines, while 'titillating' the roof to test for a fall and moving the hydraulic chocks, as heavy as cannons, which propped up the roof.

They reminded me of troops bringing up artillery under fire. Their lives depended upon how they worked; and in every sense – the clipped commands, the tense, planned assault on a stubborn adversary, the degradation of a filthy wet trench and the spirit of comradeship, of watching out for each other – this was another kind of front line.

John Pilger

ACTIVITY

1 What do you think the purpose of each piece of writing is? Examine the ways in which each writer uses language in different ways in order to achieve his effects. Refer to specific details of language use and its effects in your answer.
2 Write an essay comparing the two texts. You should consider:
    • language, form and structure
    • the ways in which the writers use the genre of their choice to express their thoughts and feelings
    • the writers' attitudes towards their subject matter.

Tragic Scenes:

Further activities

1 From your own reading select two pieces of writing that deal with a tragic theme. Compare these two pieces with one or two examples from the selection given here.
2 Choose any three of the pieces as a starting point to examine ways in which writers of different eras have written about a tragic theme.
3 Think about the texts you have studied for your course. Have any of them had tragic elements? If so, make notes on the ways in which the writers have explored their chosen topics.

8

The Comic Perspective

In this unit we will look at some of the ways in which writers try to make us laugh – the ways in which they create humour in their writing. Writing to make the reader laugh can be an end in itself. For example, Wendy Cope's poem *Making Cocoa for Kingsley Amis* would seem to have humour as its only goal:

It was a dream I had last week
And some kind of record seemed vital.
I knew it wouldn't be much of a poem
But I love the title.

Of course, much longer poems can take as their only or primary aim the creation of humour. In other cases, however, the humour may form part of a larger whole. In a Shakespearian comedy, the 'comic' element is only one of many elements in the play as a whole. Certainly there will be comic scenes, comic incidents and amusing dialogue, but the play's aim will be to do much more than simply 'amuse'. In this unit, we will not be concerned with the 'aim' of the work overall but with the ways in which writers use language in the extracts we look at in order to achieve the effects they want – in this case, to amuse the reader.

Writers can use language in many ways in order to achieve this, of course. Here are some points you might like to bear in mind:

- The tone in which the piece is written can be amusing – this can be closely tied up with the 'voice' adopted by the writer.
- The humour could stem from the events described.
- The characters might be the source of amusement.
- The writer might use slapstick, ridiculous or fantastic situations or characters, or use exaggeration to create a comic effect.
- The words themselves might be the source of the amusement – through punning, wordplay or overall effects created through techniques such as riddles, rhymes or limericks.
- One of the more literary forms of humorous writing is where one writer imitates but exaggerates the style of another writer – this is called parody, and we will look at some examples later in the unit.

These are clearly just a few examples of the ways in which writers can use words to amuse us. In examining the pieces that follow, always look for a range of features or techniques – often the overall effect of a piece of writing results from a combination of different techniques.

Lucky Jim

Extract A is taken from a novel by Kingsley Amis called *Lucky Jim*. The Jim of the title is Jim Dixon, a university lecturer in history, but he has not been so lucky here. He had been invited to join a group of others at the home of his professor, Professor Welch, for an intellectual weekend of part-singing, play-reading, recitations and chamber music. On the first evening Jim gets very drunk. Here is Amis's description of him as he awakes the next morning.

ACTIVITY

Read the extract carefully.
1 Amis has clearly tried to amuse his reader here. Make a note of the different techniques he has used in order to do this.
2 Pick out any parts of the description that you find particularly funny, and examine why you have found them effective.
3 Try writing your own amusing account of an incident you have experienced, or create one by using your imagination.

Dixon was alive again. Consciousness was upon him before he could get out of the way; not for him the slow, gracious wandering from the halls of sleep, but a summary, forcible ejection. He lay sprawled, too wicked to move, spewed up like a broken spider-crab on the tarry shingle of the morning. The light did him harm, but not as much as looking at things did; he resolved, having done it once, never to move his eye-balls again. A dusty thudding in his head made the scene before him beat like a pulse. His mouth had been used as a latrine by some small creature of the night, and then as its mausoleum. During the night, too, he'd somehow been on a cross-country run and then been expertly beaten up by secret police. He felt bad.

He reached out for and put on his glasses. At once he saw that something was wrong with the bedclothes immediately before his face. Endangering his chance of survival, he sat up a little, and what met his bursting eyes roused to a frenzy the timpanist in his head. A large, irregular area of the turned-back part of the blanket was missing; an area about the size of the palm of his hand in the main part of the top blanket was missing. Through the three holes, which, appropriately enough, had black borders, he could see a dark brown mark on the second blanket. He ran a finger round a bit of the hole in the sheet, and when he looked at his finger it bore a dark-grey stain. That mean ash; ash meant burning; burning must mean cigarettes. Had this cigarette burnt itself out on the blanket? If not, where was it now? Nowhere on the bed; nor in it. He leaned over the side, gritting his teeth; a sunken brown channel, ending in a fragment of valuable-looking rug. This made him feel very unhappy, a feeling sensibly increased when he looked at the bedside table. This was marked by two black, charred grooves, greyish and shiny in parts, lying at right angles and stopping well short of the ashtray, which held a single used match. On the table were two unused matches; the remainder lay with the empty cigarette packet on the floor. The bakelite mug was nowhere to be seen.

Had he done all this himself? Or had a wayfarer, a burglar, camped out in his room? Or was he the victim of some Horla fond of tobacco? He thought that on the whole he must have done it himself, and wished he hadn't. Surely this would mean the loss of his job, especially if he failed to go to Mrs Welch and confess what he'd done, and he knew already that he wouldn't be able to do that. There was no excuse which didn't consist of the inexcusable: an incendiary was no more pardonable when revealed as a drunkard as well – so much of a drunkard, moreover, that obligations to hosts and fellow-guests and the counter-attraction of a chamber-concert were as nothing compared with the lure of the drink. The only hope was that Welch wouldn't notice what his wife would presumably tell him about the burning of the bedclothes. But Welch had been known to notice things, the attack on his pupil's book in that essay, for example. But that had really been an attack on Welch himself; he couldn't much care what happened to sheets and blankets which he wasn't actually using at the time. Dixon remembered thinking on an earlier occasion that to yaw drunkenly round the Common Room in Welch's presence screeching obscenities, punching out the window-panes, fouling the periodicals, would escape Welch's notice altogether, provided his own person remained inviolate. The memory in turn reminded him of a sentence in a book of Alfred Beesley's he'd once glanced at: 'A stimulus cannot be received by the mind unless it serves some need of the organism.' He began laughing, an action he soon modified to a wince.

Kingsley Amis

Here are some of the things that you might have noted:

- the short unusual opening sentence – 'Dixon was alive again'
- the use of antithesis in the description of the way he awakens – 'Not for him the slow, gracious wandering from the halls of sleep, but a summary, forcible ejection'
- the use of metaphors and similes – 'He lay sprawled, too wicked to move, spewed up like a broken spider-crab on the tarry shingle of the morning'
- exaggeration – eg of the effects of light, how his mouth felt, the beating by the secret police, and so on
- the build-up of description culminating in the discovery of the burnt blankets.

Notes from a Small Island

Now look at this extract from *Notes From a Small Island* by the American writer Bill Bryson. Unlike *Lucky Jim*, this book is not a novel; it is a description of a tour Bryson took around the British Isles, in which he focuses on the idiosyncrasies of the British people. As a genre it is probably best described as travel writing, but Bryson is well known as a humorous writer and it is clear that he intends to portray his various experiences in an amusing light.

The way I see it, there are three reasons never to be unhappy.

First, you were born. This in itself is a remarkable achievement. Did you know that each time your father ejaculated (and frankly he did it quite a lot) he produced roughly twenty-five million spermatozoa – enough to repopulate Britain every two days or so? For you to have been born, not only did you have to be among the few batches of sperm that had even a theoretical chance of prospering – in itself quite a long shot – but you then had to win a race against 24,999,999 or so wriggling contenders, all rushing to swim the English Channel of your mother's vagina in order to be the first ashore at the fertile egg of Boulogne, as it were. Being born was easily the most remarkable achievement of your whole life. And think: you could just as easily have been a flatworm.

Second, you are alive. For the tiniest moment in the span of eternity you have the miraculous privilege to exist. For endless eons you were not. Soon you will cease to be once more. That you are able to sit here right now in this one never-to-be-repeated moment, reading this book, eating bon-bons, dreaming about hot sex with that scrumptious person from accounts, speculatively sniffing your armpits, doing whatever you are doing – just *existing* – is really wondrous beyond belief.

Third, you have plenty to eat, you live in a time of peace and 'Tie a Yellow Ribbon Round the Old Oak Tree' will never be the number one again.

If you bear these things in mind, you will never be truly unhappy – though in fairness I must point out that if you find yourself alone in Weston-super-Mare on a rainy Tuesday evening you may come close.

It was only a little after six when I stepped from the Exeter train and ventured into the town, but already the whole of Weston appeared to be indoors beyond drawn curtains. The streets were empty, dark and full of slanting rain. I walked from the station through a concrete shopping precinct and out on to the front where a black unseen sea made restless whooshing noises. Most of the hotels along the front were dark and empty, and the few that were open didn't look particularly enticing. I walked a mile or so to a cluster of three brightly lit establishments at the far end of the promenade and randomly selected a place called the Birchfield. It was fairly basic, but clean and reasonably priced. You could do worse, and I have.

I gave myself a cursory grooming and wandered back into town in search of dinner and diversion. I had an odd sense that I had been here before, which patently I had not. My only acquaintance with Weston was that John Cleese had once told me (I'm not really dropping names; I was interviewing him for a newspaper article; he is a jolly nice fellow, by the way) that he and his parents lived in a flat in Weston, and that when they moved out Jeffrey Archer and his parents moved in, which I thought was kind of remarkable – the idea of these two boys in short trousers saying hello and then one of them going on to greatness. What made Weston feel familiar was, of course, that it was just like everywhere else. It had Boots and Marks & Spencer and Dixons and W. H. Smith and all the rest of it. I realized with a kind of dull ache that there wasn't a single thing here that I hadn't seen a million times already.

I went into a pub called the Britannia Inn which was unfriendly without being actually hostile, and had a couple of lonely pints, then ate at a Chinese restaurant, not because I craved Chinese but because it was the only place I could find open. I was the only customer. As I quietly scattered rice and sweet and sour sauce across the tablecloth, there were some rumbles of thunder and, a moment later, the heavens opened – and I mean opened. I have seldom seen it rain so hard in England. The rain spattered the street like a shower of ball-bearings and within minutes the restaurant window was wholly obscured with water, as if someone were running a hose over it. Because I was a long walk from my hotel, I spun out the meal, hoping the weather would ease off, but it didn't, and eventually I had no choice but to step out into the rainy night.

I stood beneath a shop awning next door and wondered what to do. Rain battered madly on the awning and rushed in torrents through the gutters. All along the road it poured over the sides of overstretched gutters and fell to the pavement in an endless clatter. With my eyes closed it sounded like I was in the midst of some vast, insane tap-dancing competition. Pulling my jacket above my head, I waded out into the deluge, then sprinted across the street and impulsively took refuge in the first bright, open thing I came to – an amusement arcade. Wiping my glasses with a bandanna, I took my bearings. The arcade was a large room full of brightly pulsating machines, some of them playing electronic tunes or making unbidden *kerboom* noises, but apart from an overseer sitting at a counter with a drooping fag and a magazine, there was no-one in the place so it looked eerily as if the machines were playing themselves.

With the exception of penny falls and those crane things that give you three microseconds to try to snatch a stuffed animal and in which the controls don't actually correspond to the movements of the grabber bucket, I don't understand arcade games at all. Generally I can't even figure out where to insert the money or, once inserted, how to make the game start. If by some miracle I manage to surmount these two obstacles, I invariably fail to recognize that the game has come to life and that I am wasting precious seconds feeling in remote coin-return slots and searching for a button that says 'Start'. Then I have thirty confused seconds of being immersed in some frantic mayhem without having the faintest idea what's going on, while my children shout, 'You've just blown up Princess Leila, you stupid shit!' and then it says 'Game Over'.

This is more or less what happened to me now. For no reason that I can possibly attach a rational explanation to, I put 50p in a game called Killer Kickboxer or Kick His Fucking Brains Out or something like that, and spent about a minute punching a red button and waggling a joystick while my character – a muscular blond fellow – kicked at drapes and threw magic discs into thin air while a series of equally muscular but unscrupulous Orientals assaulted him with kidney chops and flung him to the carpet.

I had a strange hour in which I wandered in a kind of trance feeding money into machines and playing games I couldn't follow. I drove racing cars into bales of hay and obliterated friendly troops with lasers and unwittingly helped zombie mutants do unspeakable things to a child. Eventually I ran out of money and stepped out into the night. I had just a moment to note that the rain had eased a little and that the street was flooded, evidently from a clogged drain, when a red Fiesta sped through the puddle at great speed and unusually close to the kerb, transferring nearly all the water from the puddle and on to me.

To say that I was drenched barely hints at my condition. I was as soaked as if I had fallen into the sea. As I stood there spluttering and gasping, the car slowed, three close-cropped heads popped out the windows, shouted some happy greeting along the lines of 'Nyaa-nyaa, nyaa-nyaa!' and sped off. Glumly, I walked back along the prom, squelching with each step and shivering with cold. I don't wish to reduce this cheery chronicle to pathos, but I had only recently recovered from a fairly serious bout of pneumonia. I won't say that I nearly died, but I was ill enough to watch *This Morning with Richard and Judy*, and I certainly didn't want to be in that condition again. To add to my indignity, the Fiesta came past on a victory lap and its pleasure-starved occupants slowed to offer me another triumphal 'Nyaa-nyaa' before speeding off into the night with a screech and a brief, uncontrolled fishtail slide that unfortunately failed to bury them in a lamppost.

Bill Bryson

ACTIVITY

1 Make notes on the techniques Bryson uses in this extract to achieve a comic or amusing effect.
2 How effective do you find each technique?
3 Write an essay in which you discuss Bryson's use of language and how successful it is in achieving comic effects and amusing his readers.

Student response

Here is one student's answer to the essay question on *Notes From a Small Island*.

Throughout the extract, Bryson uses methods such as adding his own personal comment or thoughts to situations he finds himself in such as his comment on the youths who splashed him as he describes their car going into '. . . uncontrolled fishtail slide that unfortunately failed to bury them in a lamppost'. This seems to be an effective way in which Bryson can add a sometime ironic or witty comment to familiar situations.

Also a technique used by Bryson in the extract is to use familiar situations and popular culture in order to make jokes and familiarize the reader with the situation: 'I was ill enough to watch "This Morning with Richard and Judy", and I certainly didn't want to be in that condition again.'

By letting us know what he is thinking as well as what actually happens, Bryson allows himself to add his opinions and views which are usually funny. For example when he goes into the arcade and begins to play a game, 'I have thirty confused seconds of being immersed in some frantic mayhem without having the faintest idea what's going on'.

Sometimes when making a point, Bryson will add a funny comment in brackets. This is a way of sharing a joke, as in '(frankly he did it quite a lot)' when referring to someone's father ejaculating. This technique can be very effective and combines well with Bryson's chatty and informal style of writing – an informality which allows him to make jokes and add elements of humour to his writing.

Secondly, his descriptions are of great importance. The way he uses linguistic techniques, such as similes, allows the reader to actually picture the events and places he is describing – 'The rain spattered the street like a shower of ball bearings.' When describing the video arcade Bryson gives descriptions of the deserted place and vivid 'brightly pulsating machines, some of them playing electronic tunes or making unbidden kerboom noises . . .'

He uses throughout words and comparisons that will be familiar to his readers. These allow readers to form vivid ideas and pictures of events and the way Bryson feels about them.

Bryson sets out in 'Notes From a Small Island' to portray his various experiences in an amusing light. The way that this would be most evident would be in the language used. Perhaps most importantly, throughout the extract, Bryson writes in a colloquial and informal manner. This way of writing means the reader can assume Bryson is talking to them the way he would normally. This means it is easier for Bryson to include jokes and light-hearted comments in his writing. This method is used successfully in the text so that the reader can feel relaxed and be affected by the humour to a greater degree.

An important way of increasing the effectiveness of his comic elements is achieved through Bryson using vivid descriptions of sights, smells and events. This helps to make the experience more vivid for the reader because they are able to picture the places Bryson is visiting and therefore find the humorous incidents and descriptions easier to believe in. The uses of similes, like 'The rain spattered the street like a shower of ball bearings' help to re-create the experience in the mind of the reader. This kind of vivid description is particularly evident when Bryson goes to visit the amusement arcade and he describes the lights and sounds of the machines

Bryson is often very cynical in his observations of the places he is visiting and seems to like mocking them. However, this is always done with an element of comedy and lightheartedness which the reader can understand and find amusing. Overall Bryson uses language to create comic or amusing effects throughout this extract and this is done effectively and has the desired amusing effect on the reader.

Michael

Examiner's comments

This is a sound response to the question and reveals the following positive features:

- The student maintains focus on the task throughout.
- He identifies a range of relevant features in terms of Bryson's technique.
- He identifies examples of these techniques and usually gives specific evidence to illustrate the point.
- He considers the effect that the language has on the reader and is aware that the writer is shaping his material in order to create a particular range of effects.
- The essay is reasonably well structured, although it could be more fluent in places.
- Overall the student shows a good understanding of the passage and the ways in which Bryson uses language to achieve his effects.

Reading Scheme

Earlier in the unit we mentioned **parody**, a 'literary' form where one writer mimics and exaggerates the style of another. The poet Wendy Cope, as well as being recognized for the quality of her own verse, is also renowned as a parodyist of other forms of writing and the works of other writers.

In the following poem she parodies the kind of reading schemes that used to be commonly used in infant schools to teach young children to read.

Here is Peter. Here is Jane. They like fun.
Jane has a big doll. Peter has a ball.
Look, Jane, look! Look at the dog! See him run!

Here is Mummy. She has baked a bun.
Here is the milkman. He has come to call.
Here is Peter. Here is Jane. They like fun.

Go Peter! Go Jane! Come, milkman, come!
The milkman likes Mummy. She likes them all.
Look, Jane, look! Look at the dog! See him run!

Here are the curtains. They shut out the sun.
Let us peep! On tiptoe Jane! You are small!
Here is Peter. Here is Jane. They like fun.

I hear a car, Jane. The milkman looks glum.
Here is Daddy in his car. Daddy is tall.
Look, Jane, look! Look at the dog! See him run!

Daddy looks very cross. Has he a gun?
Up milkman! Up milkman! Over the wall!
Here is Peter. Here is Jane. They like fun.
Look, Jane, look! Look at the dog! See him run!

Wendy Cope

ACTIVITY

1 From the way in which the poem is written, what conclusion do you draw about the reading schemes on which Cope bases her poem?
2 How do the poem's structure and its rhyme and rhythm patterns add to its effectiveness?
3 What does the humour of Cope's poem depend on? (You need to look at both the language and the meaning here.)
4 Try writing a poem of your own parodying any kind of writing you choose.

In the next two poems Wendy Cope parodies the styles of the nineteenth-century poet William Wordsworth, and the twentieth-century poet T. S. Eliot.

A Nursery Rhyme

as it might have been written
by William Wordsworth

The skylark and the jay sang loud and long,
The sun was calm and bright, the air was sweet,
When all at once I heard above the throng
Of jocund birds a single plaintive bleat.

And, turning, saw, as one sees in a dream,
It was a sheep had broke the moorland peace
With his sad cry, a creature who did seem
The blackest thing that ever wore a fleece.

I walked towards him on the stony track
And, pausing for a while between two crags,
I asked him, 'Have you wool upon your back?'
Thus he bespake, 'Enough to fill three bags.'

Most courteously, in measured tones, he told
Who would receive each bag and where they dwelt;
And oft, now years have passed and I am old,
I recollect with joy that inky pelt.

Wendy Cope

A Nursery Rhyme

as it might have been written
by T. S. Eliot

Because time will not run backwards
Because time
Because time will not run
                    Hickory dickory

In the last minute of the first hour
I saw the mouse ascend the ancient timepiece,
Claws whispering like wind in dry hyacinths.

One o'clock,
The street lamp said,
'Remark the mouse that races towards the carpet.'

And the unstilled wheel still turning
                    Hickory dickory
                    Hickory dickory

Dock

Wendy Cope

ACTIVITY   1 If you are not familiar with poetry written by Wordsworth or T. S. Eliot, have a look at some. If you do not have any poetry books with their poems in yourself, you could go to your local library or one at your college or school.

2 Having looked at some poems by Eliot and Wordsworth, make notes on how Wendy Cope has used language in each of poems D and E to capture the 'feel' of the poet she is parodying.

3 Now choose a poet whose works you are familiar with and write your own parody of his or her style of poetry.

Emma

Jane Austen wrote in the first half of the nineteenth century, and her novels are very much concerned with examining the social world that surrounded her. In many ways, therefore, she is noted as a social observer, but she is also noted for her wit. Her early novels, in particular, contain much that is humorous, their humour often relying on Austen's keen sense of irony. Her humour is of a subtle kind that requires close reading of the text to be fully appreciated.

Austen's humour is created primarily in four different ways:

- the exaggeration of personality – or caricature
- the juxtaposition of two incongruous elements
- irony
- the wit of her characters.

Many amusing passages from Austen's novels use several of these techniques.

Read the following passage from *Emma*. At the beginning of the novel Emma Woodhouse's devoted governess and friend, Miss Taylor, has married Mr Weston, a neighbour of the Woodhouses. In this passage, Emma's father, Mr Woodhouse, reveals his view of Miss Taylor's very happy marriage. The new Mrs Weston has received a letter from Mr Weston's son, a man famed for his polished manners.

It was, indeed, a highly-prized letter. Mrs Weston had, of course, formed a very favourable idea of the young man; and such a pleasing attention was an irresistible proof of his great good sense, and a most welcome addition to every source and every expression of congratulation which her marriage had already secured. She felt herself a most fortunate woman; and she had lived long enough to know how fortunate she might well be thought, where the only regret was for a partial separation from friends, whose friendship for her had never cooled, and who could ill bear to part with her.

    She knew that at times she must be missed; and could not think, without pain, of Emma's losing a single pleasure, or suffering an hour's ennui, from the want of her companionableness: but dear Emma was of no feeble character; she was more equal to her situation than most girls would have been, and had sense and energy and spirits that might be hoped would bear her well and happily through its little difficulties and privations. And then there was such comfort in the very easy distance of Randalls from Hartfield, so convenient for even the solitary female walking, and in Mr Weston's disposition and circumstances, which would make the approaching season no hindrance to their spending half the evenings in the week together.

Her situation was altogether the subject of hours of gratitude to Mrs Weston, and of moments only of regret; and her satisfaction – her more than satisfaction – her cheerful enjoyment was so just and so apparent, that Emma, well as she knew her father, was sometimes taken by surprise at his being still able to pity 'poor Miss Taylor,' when they left her at Randalls in the centre of every domestic comfort, or saw her go away in the evening attended by her pleasant husband to a carriage of her own. But never did she go without Mr Woodhouse's giving a gentle sigh, and saying:

'Ah! poor Miss Taylor. She would be very glad to stay.'

There was no recovering Miss Taylor – nor much likelihood of ceasing to pity her: but a few weeks brought some alleviation to Mr Woodhouse. The compliments of his neighbours were over; he was no longer teased by being wished joy of so sorrowful an event; and the wedding-cake, which had been a great distress to him, was all eat up. His own stomach could bear nothing rich, and he could never believe other people to be different from himself. What was unwholesome to him, he regarded as unfit for any body; and he had, therefore, earnestly tried to dissuade them from having any wedding-cake at all, and when that proved vain, as earnestly tried to prevent any body's eating it. He had been at the pains of consulting Mr Perry, the apothecary, on the subject. Mr Perry was an intelligent, gentlemanlike man, whose frequent visits were one of the comforts of Mr Woodhouse's life; and, upon being applied to, he could not but acknowledge, (though it seemed rather against the bias of inclination,) that wedding-cake might certainly disagree with many – perhaps with most people, unless taken moderately. With such an opinion, in confirmation of his own, Mr Woodhouse hoped to influence every visitor of the new-married pair; but still the cake was eaten; and there was no rest for his benevolent nerves till it was all gone.

There was a strange rumour in Highbury of all the little Perrys being seen with a slice of Mrs Weston's wedding-cake in their hands; but Mr Woodhouse would never believe it.

Jane Austen

ACTIVITY

1 Write a brief summary of what is being said in the extract.
2 Look at the following details of language use:
   - What is implied by the word 'recovering', at the beginning of the penultimate paragraph? Why is this ironic?
   - Why is 'pity' an unusual word to use here?
   - What incongruous ideas are juxtaposed in 'being wished joy of so sorrowful an event'?
   - What is your response to the use of the word 'distress' to describe Mr Woodhouse's reaction to the cake?

3 Mr Woodhouse is quite serious in his attempts to discourage people from eating the cake, and this makes him look ridiculous. Pick out the words and phrases that are used to make his efforts seem serious, and comment on them.
4 Some other elements of the humour of this passage come from Austen's caricature of Mr Woodhouse. What aspects of his character does she emphasize through exaggeration, and how do you respond?
5 What is implied about Mr Perry through the use of an aside (the words in brackets)?
6 Why does Austen use the word 'benevolent' to describe Mr Woodhouse's nerves?
7 Comment on the effect of the final sentence.

Bleak House

Charles Dickens is another nineteenth-century novelist. He wrote a little later in the century than Austen. Dickens, too was a great social observer, and is noted for his vivid descriptions and caricatures of people. In this extract from *Bleak House* he describes tea-time with the Smallweed family. The family consists of the grandfather, Joshua Smallweed, his wife Mrs Smallweed, and their grandchildren, the twins Judith and Bartholomew. The latter works as a clerk at a firm of solicitors. All the Smallweeds are dry and serious and lack all imagination. Even the younger ones give the impression of never having enjoyed themselves, even as children

At the present time, in the dark little parlour certain feet below the level of the street – a grim, hard, uncouth parlour, only ornamented with the coarsest of baize table-covers, and the hardest of sheet-iron tea-trays, and offering in its decorative character no bad allegorical representation of Grandfather Smallweed's mind – seated in two black horse-hair porter's chairs, one in each side of the fireplace, the superannuated Mr and Mrs Smallweed wile away the rosy hours. On the stove are a couple of trivets for the pots and kettles which it is Grandfather Smallweed's usual occupation to watch, and projecting from the chimney-piece between them is a sort of brass gallows for roasting, which he also superintends when it is in action. Under the venerable Mr Smallweed's seat, and guarded by his spindle legs, is a drawer in his chair, reported to contain property to a fabulous amount. Beside him is a spare cushion, with which he is always provided, in order that he may have something to throw at the venerable partner of his respected age whenever she makes an allusion to money – a subject on which he is particularly sensitive.

'And where's Bart?' Grandfather Smallweed inquires of Judy, Bart's twin-sister.

'He an't come in yet,' says Judy.

'It's his tea-time, isn't it?'

'No.'

'How much do you mean to say it wants then?'

'Ten minutes.'

'Hey?'

'Ten minutes.' – (Loud on the part of Judy.)

'Ho!' says Grandfather Smallweed. 'Ten minutes.'

Grandmother Smallweed, who has been mumbling and shaking her head at the trivets, hearing figures mentioned, connects them with money, and screeches, like a horrible old parrot without any plumage, 'Ten ten-pound notes!'

Grandfather Smallweed immediately throws the cushion at her.

'Drat you, be quiet!' says the good old man.

The effect of this act of jaculation is twofold. It not only doubles up Mrs Smallweed's head against the side of her porter's chair, and causes her to present, when extricated by her granddaughter, a highly unbecoming state of cap, but the necessary exertion recoils on Mr Smallweed himself, whom it throws back into *his* porter's chair, like a broken puppet. The excellent old gentleman being, at these times, a mere clothes-bag with a black skull-cap on the top of it, does not present a very animated appearance until he has undergone the two operations at the hands of his granddaughter, of being shaken up like a great bottle, and poked and punched like a great bolster. Some indication of a neck being developed in him by these means, he and the sharer of his life's evening again sit fronting one another in their two porter's chairs, like a couple of sentinels long forgotten on their post by the Black Serjeant, Death.

Judy the twin is worthy company for these associates. She is so indubitably sister to Mr Smallweed the younger, that the two kneaded into one would hardly make a young person of average proportions; while she so happily exemplifies the before-mentioned family likeness to the monkey tribe, that, attired in a spangled robe and cap, she might walk about the table-land on the top of a barrel-organ without exciting much remark as an unusual specimen. Under existing circumstances, however, she is dressed in a plain, spare gown of brown stuff.

Judy never owned a doll, never heard of Cinderella, never played at any game. She once or twice fell into children's company when she was about ten years old, but the children couldn't get on with Judy, and Judy couldn't get on with them. She seemed like an animal of another species, and there was instinctive repugnance on both sides. It is very doubtful whether Judy knows how to laugh. She has so rarely seen the thing done, that the probabilities are strong the other way. Of anything like a youthful laugh, she certainly can have no conception. If she were to try one, she would find her teeth in her way; modelling that action of her face, as she unconsciously modelled all its other expressions, on her pattern of sordid age. Such is Judy.

Charles Dickens

ACTIVITY

1 How do you respond to this description of the Smallweeds?
2 Now look carefully at the language that Dickens uses to describe them.
   - Make a list of all the words he uses to describe them that have negative connotations.
   - Make a list of all the words he uses to describe them that have positive connotations.
   - You will probably have found quite a number in each category. Why is it, then, that the positive words do not create a positive impression in our minds?
3 Make a note of any particularly 'difficult' words that you are not familiar with, which Dickens uses in his description. Look up the meaning of these words in a dictionary if you need to. Sometimes he might use a rather grand or elevated way of phrasing something rather than express it in simple terms. What is the effect of this technique? Does it add any humour? Think about this in relation to **tone** and **subject**.
4 Now look at Dickens's use of figurative language in this extract. Make a list of the similes and the metaphors he uses, and comment on the effectiveness of each one in terms of contributing to the humour of the piece.

The Rivals

The next extract is from the play *The Rivals*, an eighteenth-century comedy written by Richard Sheridan. In this extract Sir Anthony Absolute discusses a match between his son, Jack, and Mrs Malaprop's niece and ward, a headstrong and wilful young woman called Lydia, who refuses absolutely to co-operate with her aunt's wishes.

Act I Scene 2

Mrs Malaprop:	There's a little intricate hussy for you!
Sir Anthony:	It is not to be wondered at, Ma'am – all this is the natural consequence of teaching girls to read. Had I a thousand daughters, by heaven! I'd as soon have them taught the black art as their alphabet!
Mrs Malaprop:	Nay, nay, Sir Anthony, you are an absolute misanthropy!
Sir Anthony:	In my way hither, Mrs Malaprop, I observed your niece's maid coming forth from a circulating library! She had a book in each hand – they were half-bound volumes, with marble covers! From that moment I guessed how full of duty I should see her mistress!
Mrs Malaprop:	Those are vile places, indeed!
Sir Anthony:	Madam, a circulating library in a town is as an ever-green tree of diabolical knowledge! It blossoms through the year! And depend on it, Mrs Malaprop, that they who

are so fond of handling the leaves, will long for the fruit at last.

Mrs Malaprop: Well, but Sir Anthony, your wife, Lady Absolute, was fond of books.

Sir Anthony: Aye – and injury sufficient they were to her, Madam. But were I to choose another helpmate, the extent of her erudition should consist in her knowing her simple letters, without their mischievous combinations; and the summit of her science be – her ability to count as far as twenty. The first, Mrs Malaprop, would enable her to work A.A. upon my linen; and the latter would be quite sufficient to prevent her giving me a shirt, No.1 and a stock, No.2.

Mrs Malaprop: Fie, fie, Sir Anthony, you surely speak laconically!

Sir Anthony: Why, Mrs Malaprop, in moderation, now, what would you have a woman know?

Mrs Malaprop: Observe me, Sir Anthony. I would by no means wish a daughter of mine to be a progeny of learning; I don't think so much learning becomes a young woman; for instance – I would never let her meddle with Greek, or Hebrew, or Algebra, or Simony, or Fluxions, or Paradoxes, or such inflammatory branches of learning – neither would it be necessary for her to handle any of your mathematical, astronomical, diabolical instruments; but, Sir Anthony, I would send her, at nine years old, to a boarding-school, in order to learn a little ingenuity and artifice. Then, Sir, she should have a supercilious knowledge in accounts; and as she grew up, I would have her instructed in geometry, that she might know something of the contagious countries; but above all, Sir Anthony, she should be mistress of orthodoxy, that she might not mis-spell and mispronounce words so shamefully as girls usually do; and likewise that she might reprehend the true meaning of what she is saying. This, Sir Anthony, is what I would have a woman know; and I don't think there is a superstitious article in it.

Sir Anthony: Well, well, Mrs Malaprop, I will dispute the point no further with you; though I must confess, that you are a truly moderate and polite arguer, for almost every third word you say is on my side of the question. But, Mrs Malaprop, to the more important point in debate – you say, you have no objection to my proposal.

Mrs Malaprop: None, I assure you. I am under no positive engagement with Mr Acres, and as Lydia is so obstinate against him, perhaps your son may have better success.

Sir Anthony: Well, Madam, I will write for the boy directly. He knows not a syllable of this yet, though I have for some time had the proposal in my head. He is at present with his regiment.

Mrs Malaprop:	We have never seen your son, Sir Anthony; but I hope no objection on his side.
Sir Anthony:	Objection! – let him object if he dare! No, no, Mrs Malaprop, Jack knows that the least demur puts me in a frenzy directly. My process was always very simple – in their younger days, 'twas 'Jack, do this' – if he demurred – I knocked him down – and if he grumbled at that – I always sent him out of the room.
Mrs Malaprop:	Aye, and the properest way, o'my conscience! – nothing is so conciliating to young people as severity. Well Sir Anthony, I shall give Mr Acres his discharge, and prepare Lydia to receive your son's invocations; and I hope you will represent her to the Captain as an object not altogether illegible.
Sir Anthony:	Madam, I will handle the subject prudently. Well, I must leave you – and let me beg you, Mrs Malaprop, to enforce this matter roundly to the girl; take my advice – keep a tight hand – if she rejects the proposal – clap her under lock and key: and if you were just to let the servants forget to bring her dinner for three or four days, you can't conceive how she'd come about! (*Exit* **Sir Anthony**)

Richard Sheridan

ACTIVITY

1. Basing your answer on extract F and extract H, write a comparison of the ways the writers present their characters. Comment on the key differences or similarities of technique as you see it.
2. By comparing **two poems** from extracts C–E with extracts G and H, examine the range of comic techniques that these writers employ and comment on their effectiveness. You should consider:
   - language, form and structure
   - the ways the writers use the genre of their choice to express thoughts and feelings
   - attitudes to the society of the time
   - influences upon the writers
   - the gender of the writers.

The Comic Perspective:

Further activities

1 Choosing three extracts as a starting point, examine some of the ways in which writers of different eras show a different attitude towards their writing and the creation of a 'comic effect'.

2 Collect your own examples of what you consider to be effective comic writing, making notes on the success of each one and how that success is achieved.

3 Think about the texts you have studied on your course that have comic passages, themes or ideas. Make a collection of them, noting how the writer creates a sense of comedy in each case.